BLESSEDS JACINTA AND FRANCISCO OF FATIMA

CECÍLIA CALABRESI

Blesseds
JACINTA
and
FRANCISCO
of Fatima

ST PAULS

Original Title: *Jacinta e Francisco*
© 2000, PAULUS Editora
  Estrada de S.Paulo
  26850704 APELAÇÃO (Portugal)

Translated by Sr M. Colm McCool, O.P.

ST PAULS Publishing
187 Battersea Bridge Road, London SW11 3AS, UK
www.stpauls.ie

Copyright (English translation) © STPAULS UK 2003

ISBN 085439 653 5

Set by TuKan DTP, Fareham, UK
Printed by Interprint Ltd., Marsa, Malta

ST PAULS is an activity of the priests and brothers
of the Society of St Paul who proclaim the Gospel
through the media of social communication

Contents

Preface		7
Ch.1	In Aljustrel	9
Ch.2	The first apparition	15
Ch.3	The apparitions	24
Ch.4	Collabo rating with God	48
Ch.5	Conversations with heaven	58
Ch.6	Like a burning lamp	85
Ch.7	The road to Calvary	90
Ch.8	Jacinta's last days	101

Preface

Jacinta and Francisco, the two privileged children of Our Lady. Certainly, the young readers of this book are not going to think that it is something to be won, that is to say a prize, to see Our Lady. Rather it is a privilege granted to very few, and we can even be saints, great saints at that, without ever knowing what visions are, but when they are granted, they are a great help.

Our Lady appeared to Jacinta and Francisco six times, in Fatima, at the Cova da Iria.

The little shepherds, if they were good before the visions, afterwards became even better.

However, they did not give up playing in the fresh air, running after butterflies, because joy is not the opposite of holiness, in fact it may even be a sign of it. But they did two things which, if you learn to do, could make you saints too: they prayed more often and more fervently and they made many sacrifices, overcoming themselves every day.

Francisco, "after saying many Rosaries every day", was the first to go to heaven. Jacinta followed him about two years afterwards.

From the life of Jacinta, especially, you may

draw some examples which, I am certain, will help you very much.

Read about them with love; imitate them as well as you can, and then, one day, you will be admitted to the eternal vision of the most beautiful face of the Virgin Mary.

Cecília Calabresi

Chapter 1
In Aljustrel

Portugal, in the spring of 1916

Fatima is a village in the hills almost in the centre of Portugal. It has small houses, sheltered by the branches of fig trees, often kissed by the sun, which envelops persons and objects in blazing heat.

Aljustrel is in the locality of Fatima, in the Serra d'Aire.

Here, the soil is poor, the hills are bare, and the countryside is lonely and sad. Along the slopes of the hills, the flocks graze, among olive trees, oaks and holm-oaks.

The people are humble and timid and live mostly in the fertile valleys or on the surrounding hillsides. The men dress simply: a peaked cap, short padded jacket, wide trousers; they work in the fields and do not envy the rich in the city.

The women stay at home: weaving, spinning, keeping everything clean and tidy, teaching the children their prayers. They have a simple hairstyle with a parting in the middle. They wear a wide skirt under a jacket tied at the waist and finishing in a wide black band. In summer, a straw hat is worn over the usual headscarf.

The boys leave their house early in the morning, carrying their lunch in a saucepan and leading the flock to graze on the nearby hillsides, returning home at the evening *Angelus*. Only then can it be said that the family are together. After a simple supper, gathered joyfully around the table, they all say the Rosary. The father begins and the mother and children answer all together. When the prayers are over, the little ones kiss their parents' hands, asking their blessing, and go off to bed.

The youngest children

In this Christian atmosphere, Francisco was born in Aljustrel on 11 June 1908.

Nine brothers and sisters had preceded him in the family and he was not to be the last. In fact, almost two years afterwards, on 11 March 1910, in the home of Manuel and Olímpia Marto, the first cry of the last child was heard: Jacinta, inseparable companion of little Francisco.

Lúcia was the youngest of the six children of António and Maria Rosa dos Santos and lived quite close to her two cousins who were devoted to her. In the early days Lúcia was not much drawn to them: Jacinta was a good child, but rather sensitive and quite touchy, compared to Lúcia's more balanced character; Francisco, naturally peace-loving and compliant, was the complete opposite to Lúcia who was uninhibited and lively. But later, all three became close friends.

By the well

On the property of the Santos family, hidden among almond trees, olive trees and chestnuts, there was a well, enclosed by large flagstones. This was the scene of a great many simple games. The three children loved to go there.

Jacinta would sit on the edge of the well. Independent and lively, she would then announce the name of the game they were going to play. She had to be allowed to choose, otherwise she would sulk, and spoil any fun for Francisco and Lúcia for days.

At other times, it was Lúcia who told 'little stories', heard around the hearth, or from the catechism lessons her mother taught her on winter evenings. Francisco preferred to listen and agree.

With others

With the other children Francisco was docile too. He took part in their games; he was lively and interested, but not very enthusiastic.

"I'll go, but I'm quite sure I'll lose," he would say.

He very rarely won, because the other boys, on the lookout for ways of cheating, knew how to find a thousand ways of changing the results and convincing Francisco that he was mistaken, that he hadn't won and that, therefore, the game had to be played again. Francisco would give in without further resistance.

"Do you think you've won? That's all right. It doesn't matter."

At other times, however, he would withdraw from the game.

"Why?" one of them who really liked playing with him would ask.

"Because", he would answer simply, "you boys are not good." Or: "Because I don't want to play any more."

A sign that things were not all that they should be.

Ready to forgive

If any boy deceived him and took advantage of his goodness to steal something from him, Francisco forgave him without demanding restitution. This happened when one day he went to Lúcia's house with a scarf. He had to show it off because Our Lady's face was painted on it and he had got it from a sanctuary. A group of children gathered around Francisco. The scarf passed from hand to hand, coveted by many. But soon afterwards, it disappeared, having 'flown' into the pocket of one of those present. There was, naturally, an argument.

"Thief!" said one.

"It's Francisco's!" added another, attempting to drag it from the hands of the would-be owner who threatened to do damage with his teeth.

Things might have ended badly, if Francisco had not gone to the little thief and said quite calmly:

"All right, all right, I'll give it to you. Don't be upset."

How different from Jacinta, who always wanted to win with everyone and in everything!

"He didn't seem to be Jacinta's brother," wrote Lúcia, "except for his features."

In the open air

But if Francisco was not much given to playing games with other boys, nevertheless he loved running about outside, up the hills, through the meadows carpeted with flowers of all colours. He dipped his hands in the springs, played his pipe in the shade of a chestnut tree or under an oak, competing with the song of the birds.

And what a joy it was for him, gentle little boy that he was, to pick up with his staff the lizards and adders that he met along the road, and take them to drink the sheep's milk which he poured into a cavity in the stones! To discover in the thickets and burrows, hares, moles, foxes, hedgehogs and other animals was his greatest delight.

The birds' friend

Francisco, like Jacinta and Lúcia, showed the sturdy character typical of mountain peoples, but in his case he also had a delicate and gentle spirit.

While the others were chasing butterflies, he would talk to the birds of the air, giving them some of his lunch, protecting their nests. "Poor little things," he would say, calling them by name, "you're starving with hunger. Come on, have something to eat."

One day he asked a friend to lend him the money

to buy a goldfinch, which a boy had captured in his hand. He restored the little bird's freedom, after shouting happily to it, "Watch out! Don't let yourself get caught again."

He couldn't do otherwise. The same Francisco who could pardon the little thief knew also how to protect the innocent creatures of the good God.

Chapter 2
The first apparition

The three children, their hearts as pure as the sky and the hills, their souls as transparent as crystal, spent their time in simple joys. None of them was able to read. Lúcia, the eldest, was docile. Francisco, a playful, intelligent boy, was never the first to suggest a game and always yielded more easily than Lúcia. Jacinta wore a striped skirt reaching midway down her legs, and a cotton apron under a wide blouse, caught at the waist by a girdle of the same colour. Her hair was parted in the middle and when she went to graze the flock, she tied it back with a large shawl, which came down to her waist.

Lively and spontaneous, she grew up with her brother Francisco, the two youngest of eleven children in a happy, loving home. Their mother, Olímpio de Jesus, and their father, Manuel Marto, watched over the upbringing of their children just as Rosa and António dos Santos were careful about Lúcia's.

They were not rich, but they lived on what belonged to them, their fields and their flocks, the wealth of the families around Fatima.

At the pasture

In 1915 Lúcia was just eight years old. The time for playing was almost over for her.

Her mother gave her charge of the flock.

Jacinta and Francisco asked their mother to let them go with their cousin to the pasture: but they were not allowed, because they were too small.

Thus, they had to be content with seeing her in the evenings, when they went out to the nearby threshing floor to look at the sunset. Those sparkling little stars were for them so many lights that the angels were lighting in the windows of heaven. The sun was Our Lord's lamp and the moon Our Lady's. There were, however, nights when Our Lady's lamp ran out of oil and so couldn't be seen. However, Jacinta still liked it just as well and used to say:

"I still like Our Lady's lamp better than Jesus' because it doesn't burn or blind you."

"Eh? No, Jacinta!" Francisco would retort. "No lamp is as beautiful as Our Lord's."

And they competed with one another to see who could count the most stars in the sky. This pastime however was too passive for Jacinta who demanded play and action. She had to go to the pasture with Lúcia, so along with Francisco, she asked her parents once more. This time they succeeded. Imagine how joyfully they rushed off to give Lúcia the good news!

They arranged how they would meet every day. At the time decided by their mother, they opened their own sheepfold. The first to arrive would wait for the others beside a pool at the bottom of the hill. There they would decide where to pasture the flock each day.

What a joy for the little ones!

When, early in the morning, the lively and graceful little figure of Jacinta arrived at the gate of the sheepfold, her little lambs (very few, indeed, because she could not mind many) recognised her through the gate, and when she drew back the iron bar, ran happily to her.

The three children usually went to Loca do Cabeço, an isolated and lonely place but their favourite because it abounded in flowers. Their lively games filled the grove with voices and shouts.

Jacinta loved to hear her own voice re-echoing from the foot of the valleys. Here they would be, then, seated on the hillside, shouting down the valley at the top of their voices, repeating their names which the wind took up and the echo repeated, once, twice, three times.

Jacinta often recited the 'Hail Mary', word for word, enraptured to hear the echo resounding back.

Francisco, on the other hand, preferred to amuse himself with the birds, rivalling one another in songs and sounds as they twittered in the trees. He really loved birds!

And did the children pray too? Of course! Their mothers had told them to say the Rosary every day, after their lunch; and they did so, faithfully, but play was a need for them; prayer was a duty. At their age, a good solution was soon found.

This is what they said: "Hail Mary, Hail Mary,

Hail Mary, Hail Mary..." and thus the beads slipped by. When the decade was finished, they said slowly the words: "Our Father", and in the twinkling of an eye, the Rosary was over!

A mysterious figure

One day they went to the Cabeço with three other little shepherds.

They climbed up the side of a hill, and kneeling down in the shadow of a rock began to pray as usual.

It was between April and October in the year 1915 and the First World War was at its height.

Suddenly, above the trees in the valley, which was spread out at their feet, they saw a strange white figure.

"What can it be?" they asked one another in wonder. But none of them could answer.

On the following days, they saw the mysterious figure twice; it gave them a feeling of joy and, at the same time, of fear.

What could it be? Lúcia, encouraged by her mother to draw conclusions, said that she saw something that seemed to her like "a man wrapped in a sheet", and for a long time simply laughed at it, without attaching any importance to the occurrence.

The Angel of Peace

Meanwhile the spring of 1916 arrived. The First World War claimed innumerable victims on all fronts, causing mourning in many Portuguese families.

One day Francisco had followed Lúcia and Jacinta up the slope of the Cabeço. They had finished their frugal lunch and said the Rosary in a sheltered spot, and were playing, when a gust of wind made them look up. In the olive grove, at the foot of the hill, they saw in the air a snow-white figure.

Could it be the "man in the sheet" again?

Yes, but this time he came towards them. Joy, awe, fear: they felt all three in their hearts.

But the figure, coming near to them, smiling, said to them: "Do not be afraid. I am the Angel of Peace. Pray with me." They did as he did: they knelt down, bent their foreheads to the ground and repeated what they heard the Angel saying:

"My God, I believe, I adore, I hope and I love you! I ask pardon of you for those who do not believe, do not adore, do not hope and do not love you."

Having repeated this prayer three times, the Angel rose and said:

"Pray thus. The Hearts of Jesus and Mary are attentive to the voice of your supplications."

And he disappeared.

Exhausted, completely absorbed, they kept on repeating the same prayer, as if impelled by an unknown force. And they told nobody what had happened.

The Angel appears again

One day, in the summer of the following year, the three children were playing beside the well near Lúcia's house.

Suddenly, they saw beside them the same figure.

"What are you doing?" he asked. "Pray, pray very much. The Hearts of Jesus and Mary have designs of mercy on you. Offer prayers to the Most High. I am the Guardian Angel of Portugal. Above all, accept with love the sufferings which Our Lord will send you."

Kneeling down, they prayed a long time. When they had finished, Francisco asked Lúcia: "You spoke to the Angel. What did he say to you?"

"What? Didn't you hear him too?"

"No, I saw that you were talking to somebody. I heard what you said, but nothing of what he said to you."

Speak? How could Lúcia speak, when she was so astonished and impressed by this extraordinary meeting?

"Listen, Francisco, ask me that tomorrow. Or else, ask Jacinta, if you like."

"Jacinta," called the little boy, "tell me what the Angel said."

But Jacinta gave the same answer as Lúcia: "Tomorrow."

The following day

Francisco, always calm, resigned himself. But that night for him was not like other nights. He slept fitfully and his usual night's sleep, long and peaceful, was interrupted often as he tossed and turned in his bed until at last dawn broke.

"Did you sleep well last night?" he asked Lúcia when he met her.

"Yes, what do you mean? Didn't you?"

"I thought the whole time about the Angel."

Lúcia then told him all about it. But Francisco kept on interrupting her to ask:

"And who is the Most High? And why is Our Lord offended and why does he suffer so much?"

The answer to all these questions impressed him very much.

"If Jesus is suffering, we have to console him," he thought to himself. He remained absorbed in thought for a while and then began asking questions again. This alarmed Jacinta who said to him:

"Don't tell anyone. Don't say a word about all this."

Francisco was already mature and he did not need warnings like this.

Jacinta confided to him that since all this happened, she felt she simply could not play with anybody at all.

"Neither can I!" her brother affirmed.

"But what does it matter? The Angel is more important than all that. Let's think about him."

Third apparition of the Angel

Two or three months had passed by when the Angel appeared for the third time. He was holding a chalice in his hand and suspended above it a white Host with drops of blood dripping from it. He prostrated himself and repeated three times:

"Most Holy Trinity, Father, Son and Holy Spirit, I adore you profoundly and I offer you the most precious Body, Blood, Soul and Divinity of Our Lord Jesus Christ, present in the world, in reparation for the offences committed against him. And through his most Sacred Heart and the Immaculate Heart of Mary, I beg of you the conversion of poor sinners."

He rose and gave the Host to Lúcia, and the chalice to Jacinta and Francisco, saying as he did so:

"Take the Body and Blood of Our Lord, insulted by men. Make reparation for their sins. Console your God."

The heavenly messenger thus gave them Holy Communion!

Francisco, from then on, took upon himself the task of consoling Our Lord Jesus Christ.

The Angel then vanished for ever, leaving the three children in ecstasy, absorbed in deep prayer.

The tears of God

After this vision, even Francisco dared not speak.

"It was lovely to see the Angel," he eventually said, "but ever since, I can't do anything. I can't even manage to walk. I don't know what's wrong with me."

When they realised that it was getting dark, they decided to go home.

Often, Francisco would say to the two girls that he felt God within him. But he remained absent-minded for several days because of the vision. Then, little by little, he resumed the games he used to play with Lúcia and Jacinta.

The tears of God had impressed him very much indeed. With that image in his heart, he prepared himself to be the consoler of Our Lord.

Chapter 3
The apparitions

13 May 1917, almost midday

In the Cova da Iria, not far from the village of Fatima, Jacinta and Francisco had just finished saying the Rosary.

Naturally, they had been using their 'speedy' method: "Hail Mary... Hail Mary... Hail Mary... Our Father...", the sign of the Cross twice – once at the beginning and once at the end.

Now they could go back to their games with a clear conscience, while the flock was grazing peacefully.

Lúcia was ten years old. She was the only one who had made her First Communion. Francisco, not quite nine, always wanted to sing out in the fresh air. Jacinta, at seven, loved more than anything to play. In fact, it was her idea to build a little house. Francisco was to be the mason and Lúcia and Jacinta his assistants.

The sun was shining brightly in the sky and seemed to be burning up the groves and hills. Suddenly, there was an unexpected flash of lightning. The children looked at one another in astonishment.

"That's a thunderstorm," warned Lúcia.

But there was not a single cloud on the horizon. However, it seemed best to go home before they were caught in the rain.

The sheep, led by the little shepherds, were pushing one another as they turned the corner.

Another flash of lightning made them stop. The children were terrified. As if obeying some impulse, they all turned to the left, and on a holm-oak – a common tree little more than a metre in height – they saw the radiant figure of a most beautiful Lady looking at them and beckoning.

The little shepherds wanted to run away, but the mysterious Lady drew them towards her with a motherly gesture and a wonderfully sweet voice:

"Don't be afraid: I will do you no harm."

The hearts of the children became calm at once. Jacinta and Francisco, amazed, remained silent. They simply gazed in wonderment.

She seemed to be between fifteen and eighteen years old and wore a garment of purest white, which came down to her feet. A golden cord hung around her neck. A white mantle covered her head and almost her whole person. From her hands, joined before her breast in an attitude of prayer, hung a white Rosary with a silver cross. She was not suspended in the air, but rested lightly on the holm-oak, her feet seeming to touch the leaves lightly. Her face, indescribably beautiful and gentle, was surrounded by a luminous halo and seemed veiled by a shadow of sadness.

Lúcia found the courage to ask:

"Where do you come from?"

"I come from heaven," she said, in an accent they had never heard before; tones of tenderness and kindness.

"And why have you come here?"

"I have come to ask you to come here at this same hour, six times, on the thirteenth of every month until October. Then, I will tell you who I am and what I want."

It seemed that this answer was definitive.

Lúcia, however, certainly encouraged by the kindness radiating from the beautiful vision, dared to ask once more:

"If you come from heaven, tell me: shall I go there?"

"Yes."

"And Jacinta?"

"She will go too."

"And Francisco?"

The eyes of the Apparition turned to him, in a penetrating glance of kindness and motherly reproof.

"He will go there too, but first, he must say many Rosaries."

Lúcia had not yet finished asking questions. She wanted to know the destiny of two young people who had died a short time before. And she heard from the lips of the Vision that one was in heaven, while the other was still in purgatory.

The Vision advised them always to say the Rosary with devotion, and asked them:

"Are you willing to offer sacrifices and accept the sufferings which Our Lord will send you, in reparation for so many sins by which his Divine Majesty is offended, as intercession for the conversion of sinners and to atone for blasphemies and offences committed against the Immaculate Heart of Mary?"

"Yes, we are willing," Lúcia answered enthusiastically in the name of all three.

Childish generosity which delighted Our Lady!

And she, in a motherly gesture, expressed her satisfaction. She was about to go away, but had yet another message to give them.

"You are going to have much to suffer, but the grace of God will help you and be your comfort always."

Then, opening her hands which were previously held joined, she cast over them a beam of light.

They knelt down and repeated fervently their acts of adoration and love: "Most Holy Trinity, I adore you! My God, I love you!"

The children remained lost in wonder, almost beside themselves. Had they all seen it? Yes. But while Lúcia saw and spoke, Jacinta heard but did not participate, and Francisco heard nothing but saw everything.

Their hearts overflowed with joy and experienced a sweetness they had never known before.

Day of Wonders! Now nobody, even Jacinta, wanted to play. Lúcia advised them not to tell anyone what they had seen, and they went quietly and thoughtfully home.

But Jacinta, poor child, couldn't keep quiet! Skipping with joy, full of consolation, she recalled it all, and kept exclaiming enthusiastically at every step:

"Oh! What a beautiful lady! Such a beautiful lady!"

"I suppose you're going to tell somebody," remarked Lúcia.

"No, no. I won't say anything. Don't worry."

Meanwhile, at sunset on that marvellous day the three arrived home.

"Not a word, eh? Do you understand?" Lúcia said again before they parted.

"Yes, yes!" her cousins answered.

And the sound of their voices was lost in the twilight amidst the bleating of the sheep as they returned to the fold.

Jacinta

Now that night is falling on the earth, we enter a little house, almost new, in the hamlet of Fatima.

Like all the other houses there, it consists of a ground floor only: narrow windows, set low down but letting in air and light.

In the first room, the wall of which is almost covered with religious and other pictures, blackened by smoke, there is a wooden table. At one side is the simple kitchen of country people, where the family come together in loving intimacy. Opposite the front door is the bedroom of Olímpia de Jesus and Manuel Marto. In this clean, tidy room the first cry of each of their eleven dear babies was heard.

It was in this very room that Francisco, the

second-to-last child, was born, on 11 June 1908 and then Jacinta on 11 March 1910.

Jacinta was the last of the eleven children. Graceful and very intelligent, she seemed made to love and be loved.

Her parents and her brothers and sisters cherished her. At night, when everyone was at home, they argued about who was to play with her and give her kisses.

Her mother was her teacher. When she gathered the older children around her to teach them their Catechism, Jacinta was always present and followed it all with impressive interest.

She grew up amidst the hills of her own countryside, lively and robust, quick and intelligent, simple and good. She was nevertheless a petulant character. One little argument among friends was enough to send Jacinta into a corner by herself. Calls, invitations, complaints failed to bring her back to the group. She had to be allowed to choose the game and the companion. Only then, when the whims of her rebellious little will were satisfied, would Jacinta come back, serene again and ready to sing and jump. But all this joy, vivacity and wilfulness was dominated by the desire to 'please Jesus', and it was with this strong will that Jacinta succeeded in overcoming her craze for dancing, which she loved.

She especially liked the game of 'Forfeits' – whoever lost had to do whatever the winner ordered. Jacinta nearly always gave the command to run after butterflies, catch one and bring it back; or gather a flower from the meadow, not just any flower but the one that she preferred. It was almost always a lily because Jacinta had a special fondness for this flower.

One day, however, Lúcia was the winner and Jacinta had to carry out the order. They were in Lúcia's house. One of her little brothers was writing at the table.

"Go and embrace your cousin," said Lúcia.

"No, I won't! Give me a different command. Why don't you tell me to give a kiss to Jesus up there?" and she pointed to a crucifix hanging on the wall.

"Very well. Get up on a chair and bring it to me. Then, on your knees, give it three kisses, one for Francisco, one for me and another for yourself."

"I'll give Our Lord as many kisses as you like."

Taking the crucifix, she kissed it with such devotion that Lúcia always remembered that gesture with emotion. But one thing profoundly impressed Jacinta's imagination: the cross, the nails!

"Why is Our Lord on the cross like that?" she asked.

"Because he died for us."

"Tell me how that happened."

And Lúcia explained as best she could.

The little girl was deeply moved. She wept.

"Poor Jesus! I will never commit another sin, because I don't want him to suffer on my account."

Over and over again she asked her cousin to tell her again the story of Jesus, dead for us, because she wanted to keep her resolution to love him. At other times she would leave her game, fill her apron with petals and throw them at Lúcia.

"Why are you doing that, Jacinta?"

"I'm doing what the little angels do; I'm throwing flowers at you," she laughed.

She had seen little girls dressed as angels doing that at a Eucharistic festival and had been much impressed just as she had been by a holy picture showing Jesus in the middle of a big flock of sheep, with a lamb in his arms.

Jacinta, too, used to take the little white lambs in her arms, kiss them on the forehead and caress them. One day, coming back from the pasture, instead of sending the sheep in front of her, she placed herself in the midst of them.

"Why are you there in the middle of the flock?"

"To be like Our Lord. That's what he was like in that holy picture I was given."

Once, on the feast of *Corpus Christi*, Lúcia was chosen to walk in front of the canopy in the procession. Dressed as an angel, she had to throw flowers at Jesus. It was a great joy, and Lúcia couldn't keep it to herself. She told Jacinta about it. Imagine the little one, so much a friend of flowers and of Jesus – could she resign herself to not having the same good fortune?

"I want to throw flowers at Jesus too."

It was not difficult to satisfy her. Two angels instead of one would make the ceremony more meaningful; and Jesus, for certain, would be pleased to have two hearts like theirs near him.

They practised and learned how they should throw the flowers.

"And will we see Our Lord?" asked Jacinta, her pure eyes shining with joy.

"Of course, the parish priest will bring him."

The little girl jumped for joy, and asked many times a day: "Is it the feast yet?"

When the day at last arrived, the two little angels, dressed in white and gold, walked in front of the canopy, each with her own little basket of flowers.

At the places marked, Lúcia threw her flowers gaily and lovingly.

And Jacinta? She stared at the parish priest and paid no attention to the many signs that Lúcia was making to her. When the procession was over, her little basket was still full.

"Why didn't you throw your flowers at Jesus?"

"Because I didn't see him. And you, Lúcia, did you see the Child Jesus?"

"Oh no! Didn't you know that the Child Jesus in the Host is hidden? That's how we receive him in Communion. He is there, but we don't see him."

"And do you talk to him at Communion?"

"Of course!"

"And why don't you see him?"

"Because he's hidden."

"And how is it possible that so many people receive the hidden Child Jesus at the same time? Do they each receive a little piece?"

"No! Don't you see there are many Hosts? In each one of them the Child Jesus is present, but hidden," Lúcia explained in her simple way.

Jacinta remained thoughtful. Then she said: "I am going to ask my mother to let me make my First Communion."

"The parish priest doesn't allow anyone under ten to make Holy Communion."

"But you're not ten and you've made your First Communion."

"Because I knew my doctrine well. You don't know it yet."

From then on, she was most anxious to learn it. And she asked her cousin to teach her all that was necessary in order to receive the 'Hidden Jesus'. At home, when she had finished her tasks, she would repeat the Catechism lessons, with love and perseverance.

"Mother, I saw Our Lady!"

This same Jacinta, lively and talkative, saw Our Lady. The memory of the beautiful Lady filled her with joy, but the secret weighed heavily on her heart.

"After all," she thought, "what harm would it be to tell my mother that I saw Our Lady?"

She kept quiet for some time, but could not contain herself any longer. Her heart was overflowing. So she ran to her mother, hugged her, gave her a kiss, and said:

"Mother, do you know what? Today I saw Our Lady in the Cova da Iria!"

"What are you saying. Are you crazy? Are you holy enough to see Our Lady?"

"Ah! But I did see her. And Francisco saw her too," she insisted, hanging her head sadly.

"Mother," she began again after a few moments of silence, "we have to say the Rosary every day. It's Our Lady who wants it."

It was suppertime. The family had gathered for their frugal meal. Francisco's and Jacinta's eyes were shining. While the little fellow withdrew into silence, Jacinta felt a real need to give vent to her feelings. And when interrogated, she told the whole family, in great detail, the story of the extraordinary event.

Francisco did not contradict her, but he did not add anything either. He simply confirmed Jacinta's story. He was thinking of Lúcia who had told them to keep it secret. The following day, early in the morning, he felt obliged to tell her that Jacinta had revealed everything.

As soon as the three met, Lúcia began:

"Didn't I tell you to keep quiet? You'll see now the problems we're going to have because of you."

Poor child! She wept. She didn't make any excuses. She simply said that she felt something within her that would not allow her to remain silent. And kneeling down, her hands raised, in a voice broken with sobs, she asked forgiveness:

"I did wrong, but I promise never to say anything to anyone again."

Rosaries and sacrifices

The children arrived at the place chosen for pasture that day. Jacinta sat down on a rock.

"Aren't you going to play?"

"No, I don't want to today."

"Why?"

"Because I'm thinking that the Lady told us to say the Rosary and make sacrifices for the conversion of sinners. Now, when we pray, we'll have to say the whole of the Hail Mary and the Our Father … but what about sacrifices, what will we do?"

A difficult question! Nobody knew the answer. But then Francisco, always ready with a suggestion, resolved the question:

"Look, we'll give our lunch to the sheep and make the sacrifice of not eating it."

Poor little children! Such a big sacrifice to begin with!

However, nobody asked to be exempt and the three offered it up with a real sense of satisfaction, because the pleasure we feel when we give up something is definitely greater than the satisfaction from what we give up.

Hell

Jacinta was sitting on the rock, thinking.

"That Lady also said that many souls go to hell. Hell! What is hell?"

"Hell is a very deep hole, full of demons and fire," explained Lúcia. She had been allowed to make her First Communion because she knew her

Catechism, having learned it from her mother, especially at night during Lent. "Those who commit sins and have not confessed them are thrown into that hole for ever."

"For ever?" asked the little girl in great surprise. "And they never get out?"

"Never!"

"Even after many, many years?"

"No, never. Hell lasts for ever. So does heaven."

"But doesn't anybody ever get out of hell?"

"No. I've just told you. Heaven and hell are eternal, which means they never end and last for ever."

The thought of eternity made a deep impression on Jacinta. She joined in the game again but sometimes she would leave it and start asking Lúcia questions again:

"But, listen, Lúcia, after many, many years hell never ends?"

"No. It will never end."

"And those people who are burning there never die?... and never turn into cinders?

"And if we pray very much for sinners, Our Lord won't send them to hell any more?

"And if we make many sacrifices as well?"

The answers brought her some peace.

"How good she is, that Lady who promised to bring us to heaven!" she exclaimed happily.

At other times she sat, deep in thought.

"Hell! Hell!" she would repeat. "How sorry I am for souls who go to hell! And the people are burning there like wood!"

At other times, as if she had woken from a dream, she would call the others:

"Lúcia, Francisco, pray. We have to pray very much to save souls from hell. So many fall into it!"

A storm in the family

Meanwhile, the mothers had a meeting. Lúcia, when questioned, had to reveal everything, confirming and completing what her cousins had already said. Better if she had never done so! A real storm arose in the family. Maria Rosa was convinced that it was all a lie. And she had never allowed that in any of her children. Was she then to allow it in her youngest daughter? And, what was worse, a lie of this kind? She sought advice from the parish priest. She bewailed the fact that she should be involved in such a disgrace.

"What disgrace?"

"My daughter will make us the scorn of the whole countryside."

"But if what she says is true, it will be for all of you a blessing that everyone will envy."

"If it were true! But that cannot be. The girl is becoming a liar. But it's the first time and I'll make her understand that lies are not acceptable."

Distressing hours for poor Lúcia: beatings, threats, tears, incredulity, jeers.

One morning, Maria Rosa, tired of hearing the remarks of gossips, decided to deal with the whole matter once and for all. Lúcia was to get up at once and confess that she had lied and deceived everyone.

But commands, caresses, beatings, were all in vain. She was sent out to the pasture and told to think the whole day about what her mother went on to say to her:

"If I have never yet overlooked a lie, I'm certainly not going to accept this one. Tonight you will go around to all the people you have deceived, you will confess that you lied, and ask their pardon."

"Pardon! But for what?" Lúcia asked herself, perplexed.

At the pasture, she met her cousins. "What's wrong with you? What happened to you?" they asked anxiously, seeing her in tears.

"My mother wants, at any cost, to make me say that I lied. How can I say a thing like that if it isn't true?"

"It's all your fault," Francisco said to Jacinta.

"I did wrong," she answered, ashamed, "but I promise that I'll never say anything to anyone again", and her tears fell on that holy ground.

Return to the Cova da Iria

It was the night of 12 June, the vigil of St Anthony. Enthusiasm was in the air because of the approaching feast. In all hearts were varying hopes.

Fatima would celebrate tomorrow the feast of its parish patron.

But Jacinta was not joyful because of the feast; she was thinking happily about what she expected tomorrow, the 13th. She went to her mother saying:

"Mother, don't go to St Anthony's festival

tomorrow. Come with us to the Cova da Iria to see the Lady."

"You are the one who isn't going. In any case, it's no use. Our Lady won't appear to you."

"She will, mother! Our Lady said she would appear. Of course she will appear."

"So you don't want to go to St Anthony's festival?"

"No, because St Anthony isn't beautiful. Our Lady is much more beautiful. I'm going with Francisco and Lúcia to the Cova. If, afterwards, Our Lady tells us to go to St Anthony's festival, we'll go."

The Martos didn't attach much importance to the apparitions! Early in the morning, they went off to the festival and left the children free to go to the Cova da Iria.

Preceded by about fifty people, led by curiosity more than by devotion, Francisco and Jacinta set out with Lúcia to the place of the heavenly encounter. They knelt and said the Rosary. Lúcia adjusted her shawl and the white kerchief on her head.

"Let's say another Rosary," the crowd suggested.

"No," sighed Lúcia.

"Will she be long?" asked the bystanders.

"There's the lightning. She's coming now."

Accompanied by the other two, she went to the little holm-oak where the Virgin appeared for the first time.

Ten minutes of close attention. All eyes were fixed on the three children. Everyone heard Lúcia's questions, but no one saw anything; no one heard the answers. Only one thing was observed: the leaves of the holm-oak, already fresh and green, were folded over when the apparition was gone, as if touched by the hem of Mary's mantle.

What did Lúcia say?

What did Francisco and Jacinta hear and see during these moments of mysterious conversation?

Lúcia asked Our Lady what she wanted, and in reply, heard that she wanted them to go back there on the 13th of the following month; that she wished them to say the Rosary every day and that Lúcia was to learn to read. Then she entrusted them with a secret, instructing them to tell it to no one.

Part of the secret

What was the secret? The children never revealed it. Only later, Lúcia disclosed part of it. It was Jesus in the Blessed Sacrament who allowed her partly to lift the veil from the secret of Mary, which she had faithfully and heroically kept.

Lúcia had asked the Virgin to take the three of them with her to heaven.

"Yes," she answered, "I will come soon for Francisco and Jacinta. You, however, will have to stay longer on earth. Jesus wishes to use you in order to make me known and loved."

"So I have to stay alone?" she asked sadly.

"No, my daughter, I shall never abandon you. My Immaculate Heart will always be your refuge and the way which will lead you to God."

When the vision was over, the little shepherds

returned home with the Virgin's secret in their hearts, the witnesses also with feelings of wonder.

A visit to the parish priest

Approval, expressions of astonishment, mistrust, criticisms, mockery – the three privileged children felt and suffered from all these. What made them suffer most was that among those who were hostile were the clergy – in fact, the parish priest. How was that possible? The reason is very simple: the Church always acts with great prudence concerning anything that seems to be supernatural.

In the case of the little shepherds, the fears increased. The Marto parents did not doubt the sincerity of their children but they were afraid they might have been deluded.

"I'll give you a beating, and rightly so," said their mother one day, "because you are going around deceiving people. It's your fault that so many are going to the Cova da Iria."

"We don't make anyone go there. Whoever wants to, goes; whoever doesn't want to, doesn't go. But anyone who doesn't believe may expect a punishment from God. Even you, mother, will be punished if you do not believe."

This fear of punishment had thus some power of conviction.

It wasn't like that, however, for poor Lúcia, whose mother was not so easily appeased. Convinced that her daughter was lying, she scolded her and beat her unreasonably. One night she said to her:

"Tomorrow morning we're going to Mass, and afterwards, you are going to visit the parish priest. It would do you good if he punished you. Do whatever he wants; as long as you confess that you lied, I'll be satisfied."

When they had walked a little further in silence, Lúcia's mother said:

"You will kneel down in front of him and tell him that you are a liar. You will ask pardon and he will give you a penance."

"Mother, how can I say I didn't see when I did?" Lúcia dared to object.

She told Jacinta and Francisco who said to her:

"We'll go too. The parish priest told our mother to bring us along too but she didn't say anything about it to us. Be patient! If they beat us, we'll suffer for love of Our Lord and for sinners."

They all went along. The interrogation was detailed, but without threats. The priest tried to get the children to contradict themselves, but did not succeed. Jacinta answered only in monosyllables, with her head down.

"Why?" Lúcia asked her when they came out.

"I promised not to say any more, no matter what happened; you know that."

Trick of the devil

Lúcia came away from that interview with a sad heart. The parish priest had concluded by saying:

"It doesn't seem to me as if it comes from heaven. Generally, Our Lord, when he communicates with souls, commands them to tell everything to their confessors and their parish priests. This child, on the contrary, shuts herself up in her silence. It could be a trick of the devil! The future will tell."

A trick of the devil! What a tormenting thought for poor Lúcia! But it was Jacinta who reassured her.

"No, no! It's not the devil. The devil is very ugly and lives down under the earth, in hell. That Lady, on the contrary, is very beautiful and we saw her going up to heaven."

Later, that same terrible doubt returned. By that time, Lúcia had decided it would be better to lie in order to appease her parents who continued to scold and beat her. Her cousins discovered this and dissuaded her from yielding to this temptation.

"You would be telling a real lie and that is a sin."

She kept quiet but she did not want to go back to the Cova.

"The two of you can go," she said to her cousins on the night of 12 July, "I'm never going to the Cova da Iria again. If that Lady asks you why I didn't go, tell her that I was afraid it was the devil."

Our Lady must have smiled at that fear!

Jacinta was already looking forward to the pleasure of talking to the Lady, but at the same time she felt very sad that Lúcia would not be there.

The following morning, however, impelled by some power that she could not resist Lúcia ran to meet her cousins. They were praying and weeping in their rooms:

"What? Haven't you gone? It's already time."

"Without you, we hadn't the courage to go."

"But I'm going. Come on."

And the three set out. There was a dense crowd: four or five thousand people had arrived at the scene.

The third apparition

The midday sun was at its highest and the heat was intense. The suffocating July atmosphere was even heavier because of the chirping of innumerable cicadas.

Lúcia's heart was agitated. The old doubts had returned.

"Supposing it is the devil after all?"

Immediately after the lightning, the Lady appeared, all white and shining. Lúcia just looked at her. She hadn't the courage to utter a syllable.

"Come on, Lúcia, speak! Don't you see that she's here and wants to speak to you?" urged Jacinta.

A little more confident, Lúcia asked:

"What do you want of me?"

The Lady answered:

"Come back here on the thirteenth of next month. Say the Rosary every day to obtain the end of the war, because only the Most Holy Virgin can obtain this grace for men."

She said that in October she would reveal her name and also recommended sacrifice.

"Sacrifice yourselves for sinners and say often, especially when you are making a sacrifice: 'O Jesus, it is for love of you, for the conversion of sinners and in reparation for offences committed against the Immaculate Heart of Mary.'"

Lúcia seemed very sad, and her cousins too. Those present noticed it and became fearful. When the vision was over they rushed to the three children, overwhelming them with questions. But while Lúcia tried to answer, Jacinta took refuge in the arms of her father, who, fearing that the crowd might suffocate her, took her carefully home.

Our Lady had shown the little shepherds the terrifying vision of hell: an ocean of fire. In the midst of the red flames were loathsome devils, like horrible unknown animals, transparent like burning charcoal and human beings, dark and tanned by the heat, thrown into the air by the flames and falling down again painfully amid shouts and shrieks of despair. Hell!...

Jacinta, who had been very much impressed by what her cousin had told her, was really terrified now. She would even interrupt her game to exhort the others:

"We have to pray very much in order to save souls from hell. So many go there! Why does Our Lord not show hell to sinners? If they saw it, they would not commit any more sins and they wouldn't fall into it. You, Lúcia, should tell that Lady to show them hell..."

Then as if absorbed, she kept on repeating:

"So many people go to hell! So many! So many people!"

"Don't be afraid: you're going to heaven!"

"I know that; but I'd like all those people to go there too."

Our Lady had spoken; she had given the other part of the secret.

"You have seen hell," she said, "where the souls of poor sinners go. To save them, Our Lord wishes to establish in the world devotion to my Immaculate Heart. If what I say to you is done, many souls will be saved and there will be peace. But, if not, if people do not cease offending God, the Divine Justice will send new and greater punishments...

"The present war (1914–1918) is going to end. But, if the offences against God do not stop, it will not be long, in the reign of the next Pope in fact, before a worse one will break out. When you see a night illumined by an unknown light, know that this is a sign given you by God; that he is about to punish the world for its many crimes, by means of war, famine, and persecutions of the Church and the Holy Father...

"I will come to ask for the consecration of the world to my Immaculate Heart and the Communion of Reparation on the First Saturdays for five consecutive months. If my requests are heeded, the punishment will be averted or mitigated. If not... Do not tell this to anyone."

After a few minutes she added:

"When you say the Rosary, say at the end of

each decade: 'Oh my Jesus, forgive us our sins, save us from the fire of hell, and lead all souls to heaven, especially those most in need of your mercy.'"

And she disappeared, leaving the little shepherds serious, but happy. Oh! those interviews with Our Lady, even when she recommended sacrifices, couldn't leave them sad!

Chapter 4
Collaborating with God

Have you ever noticed the different effects produced by a reflection of the sun's rays? Shining through glass, it is reflected on the ground in all the colours of the rainbow; reflected on a table, it fills the surface with white light; passing over a hand, it makes it incandescent.

The same divine light enveloped Francisco, Jacinta and Lúcia, but the reflection on each one of them was different: Lúcia was instrumental in bringing about the triumph of the Immaculate Heart of Mary; Jacinta was to make reparation for sinners; Francisco would console Our Lord.

"I enjoyed seeing the Angel," he would say to Lúcia and Jacinta, "and even more Our Lady; but what delighted me above all was to see God in that great light!"

Then he would continue: "I love Our Lord so much! He is so sad, because of so many sins! We won't commit a sin ever again, so as to console Jesus."

That was Francisco's vocation: to console Jesus. He had already been inclined this way, but after the third apparition it may be said that the inclination became a powerful attraction.

Sinners displease Our Lord

The vision of hell had terrified Jacinta. It was impossible for her to understand that hell would never end, even after "many, many years" and that "many people go there".

"Why does Our Lady not show sinners hell?" she would ask. "If they could only see it, they wouldn't commit any more sins, then they wouldn't fall into it."

And she would ask Lúcia to say that to Our Lady. But then she decided that she could do something about it and declared enthusiastically:

"If we pray a lot for sinners, if we make sacrifices for them, Our Lord won't send them to hell."

She continued to play, but without the same zest. Taken up as she was with the thought of praying for sinners, she would interrupt the game from time to time to exhort the others to pray.

"Poor sinners!" she would say. "We have to pray and make sacrifices for them."

But Francisco always put another intention in the first place:

"First, I'll console Our Lord," he would declare, "after that, I'll think about the conversion of sinners."

The idea of God being offended, and even sad, dominated him above everything else. He thought about sinners only in so far as that in offending Our Lord, they made him sad.

The animal

One day, when the three children arrived at the place of pasture, Francisco felt the need to go away and pray by himself, in the shade of a thicket. Perhaps Jacinta had invited him to pray for sinners who were falling into hell, but he had preferred to go off alone, so as to console Our Lord. For a while nothing happened, but then the other two heard Francisco's voice. He was calling for Lúcia to come and help him. They both ran at once. Francisco was on his knees, trembling.

"What happened to you? What's wrong, Francisco?"

The little boy took courage. He looked around. Not seeing anything, he said:

"There was a big animal here, one of those we saw in hell…"

As if to convince themselves, they looked all around again, then laughed at Francisco's fear.

"Do you see?" Lúcia said to him, "You don't want to think about hell so that you won't be afraid, and now, you're the first to tremble."

Francisco certainly did not want to think about hell but that was because he wanted to focus all his attention on consoling Jesus.

What is God like?

Many times, while the sheep were grazing on the fresh grass of the meadow, Francisco was immersed in thought about the vision of God. If Lúcia was not too far away, he would confide in her:

"We [alluding to the third apparition] were on fire in that light which is God and yet we were not burned. What is God like? It is impossible to describe him!"

Sometimes he would invite Jacinta and Lúcia to say the Rosary. Most times, however, he would say it alone. In fact, while the girls were playing and Francisco was walking up and down in silence, they would ask him:

"Francisco, what are you doing?"

He would raise his arm and show the Rosary which he was saying.

"Now, come and play. Afterwards, we'll all say the Rosary together," Lúcia would say.

"Afterwards... now and afterwards. Don't you remember what Our Lady said? I have to say many Rosaries."

A day of prayer and fasting

Once, when the three children arrived at the pasture, Francisco left Jacinta and Lúcia by themselves. He climbed up on a rock and asked them to allow him to be alone. They were not surprised, because he had done that often before, and so they went off to chase butterflies. What fun it was to hold them by their many-coloured wings and examine them at close quarters! But suddenly, their Angel suggested a sacrifice: let them fly away, for the sake of sinners.

The girls, also, began to enjoy self-denial. Thus occupied, they almost forgot about Francisco.

"Francisco," they called later, "aren't you going to have any lunch?"

"No. You two can have yours."

"And say the Rosary?"

"Yes. I'll come to say the Rosary. Call me again."

But when they had finished their lunch and called him, he asked them to climb up to him and pray together there. They climbed up, but could he not have picked a place a little less narrow? That rock was very hard on the knees!

"What are you doing here all this time?" they asked him.

"I'm thinking of Our Lord who is very sad because of so many sins."

To console him, Francisco had done without his lunch, spending the whole day fasting and praying, using the hard rock as a kneeler instead of the soft grass of the meadow.

That wasn't the only time that Francisco went away from Lúcia and Jacinta. Many other times he had hidden himself and had been found in prayer behind a wall or a thicket.

"Why don't you call me to pray with you?"

"Because I'd rather pray alone, so as to think better about Our Lord, who is sad because of so many sins."

Francisco is lost

One day when they had gone to graze the flock in a little pine grove, Francisco left them. This time he found it very, very difficult to go away by himself.

The pine grove was bordered on both sides by cultivated land. Lúcia had told her cousins to stay on one side while she went to the other. Jacinta, always rather dictatorial, refused:

"Not you, no. I want you near me."

Her brother didn't want to leave her and did not hide the fact.

"I want to stay with you too, but I'll offer it to Our Lord."

He went away. After a while, Lúcia thought she would ease Francisco's sacrifice.

"Jacinta," she exhorted, "go away now and keep your brother company. Poor boy! He's there all alone!" Jacinta, thinking of sinners, ran off at once.

She called, she searched and she called again. No result! Francisco is lost, she thought, worried because it was partly her fault. She returned to Lúcia in tears. Lúcia searched and called like Jacinta. They had almost lost all hope of finding him when they saw someone behind a wall. It was Francisco! Yes, there he was, praying. Lúcia had to shake him to make him hear her. Only then did Francisco waken, as if from a deep and peaceful sleep.

"Were you praying?"

"Yes. I began with the Angel's prayer and then, I kept on thinking..."

"Didn't you hear Jacinta calling you?"

"No. I didn't hear anything."

"Come on. We'll go and tell her. Poor child! She's crying because she thinks you're lost."

This contemplative solitude cost Francisco a great deal. But how would he console Our Lord if he avoided every opportunity for sacrifice?

A lunch for the poor children

"To convert sinners", "to console Our Lord", "to make reparation for offences committed against the Immaculate Heart of Mary". Here were their motives – the dominant ideas of the little shepherds. They managed to find many sacrifices in their daily lives, apparently so simple and ordinary!

One day, walking in the pasture, they met some children who lived only on what they could beg. The little shepherds had with them the bag that contained their lunch, and they were certainly hungry. Jacinta had an inspiration:

"What about giving our lunch to these poor children, for the conversion of sinners?"

No sooner said than done! They did this every time they met them, so that their days of fasting were almost continuous. When, especially towards the end of the afternoon, their stomachs protested, they tried to ease their hunger by eating roots, bitter weeds or acorns from the holm-oaks. But this was another way of making sacrifices and it was Jacinta who made a discovery and the other two happily followed.

One day when they were fasting in this way,

Francisco was climbing a holm-oak to gather acorns.

"Let's eat the acorns from the big oak," Jacinta suggested.

"But don't you think they are too bitter?"

"That's just why I eat them. In that way, we'll convert more sinners."

The others imitated her.

The godmother's hydromel

One day, Lúcia's godmother had made an excellent hydromel, which is a sweet drink, and offered a glass of it to Francisco who passed it to Jacinta and Lúcia.

"You drink first!"

Then he slipped away and even though they called him, they could not find him anywhere in the house. Jacinta and Lúcia understood. Sure of finding him at the well, they said goodbye to the godmother and went straight there. They had not been mistaken.

"Why didn't you drink any, Francisco? My godmother kept on calling you!"

"Because", he explained, "when I had the glass in my hand, I had a sudden idea: I'd make a sacrifice for Our Lord. That's why I ran away."

The voice of conscience

One day, they were playing at the well when the Marto children's mother brought them some lovely bunches of fresh grapes. They admired them and thanked her for them, but just as they were about to eat them, they heard the voice of conscience suggesting a sacrifice. When their mother left they took the grapes to the poor little children without tasting a single one.

On another occasion, they had with them a fine basket of figs, really appetising, just for themselves. And they would have eaten them if, at that moment, they had not heard the same good voice. Jacinta observed that on that particular day they had not yet made any sacrifice, so all three prepared to offer one, each with a slightly different motive, and of course Francisco did not omit his own formula – "to console Our Lord".

The proof of real love

These and many others were the sacrifices that the generous little shepherds imposed on themselves spontaneously.

As we all know, a sacrifice that is chosen by ourselves always has a secret attraction, an intimate satisfaction that makes us want to make further sacrifices.

If enthusiasm for self-denial stopped at these spontaneous sacrifices, there would never be real virtue.

It is also necessary to accept and profit by the trials Our Lord sends us.

The Hearts of Jesus and Mary, which had 'special designs' on the three little shepherds, wanted them to prove their real love, their real virtue. In fact, the proof came that August, in the fourth apparition. The little seers were missing from this encounter. How could that have happened?

Chapter 5
Conversations with heaven

At the June apparition, there were three or four thousand people present – far too many not to arouse the interest of the authorities and the Press. Whilst the Catholic newspapers recommended prudence before affirming that something supernatural was involved, the non-Catholic journals made a point of ridiculing the visions and the little ones. That was the intention, but the natural result was to spread the news about the events at Fatima over the whole of Portugal, from north to south!

Thus it was that on 13 August 1917 the whole area around the Cova da Iria was thronged with cars, bicycles, horses and more than fifteen thousand people awaiting the hour of the apparition. The sun was beating down, in that extremely hot August, but that didn't discourage the devotion of so many (nor the curiosity of a few) who hoped to see a miracle.

"Is it possible that the seers are not going to appear?"

A voice, confused at first, very clear later, passed the information from mouth to mouth: "The children were arrested by the Administrator of Vila Nova de Ourém."

There was anger, indignation and threats from the crowd. The most important people among them were getting ready to go to the Administrator's home, when some strange phenomena attracted their attention. There was an extraordinary radiance, after the usual thunder, and a very beautiful cloud rested on the holm-oak which had already been stripped of leaves and branches by pious hands. Ten minutes later, the little cloud disappeared and the crowd rightly concluded that Our Lady had not failed to come after all.

How is it possible that the Administrator had imprisoned the children? In Portugal at that time there was a law that forbade any religious demonstrations outside churches. A stickler for the law, the Administrator, who was a Mason, intervened.

Already, on Saturday 11 August, he had summoned the little seers – Francisco's and Jacinta's father appeared on their behalf. Lúcia arrived accompanied by her father. First, however, she had gone to see her cousins, and embraced them tenderly, uncertain whether she would ever see them again.

"If they want to kill you," Jacinta said at once, "tell them that Francisco and I are behind you and that we want to die too. Meanwhile, we're going over to your garden to pray very hard for you."

A long report contains Lúcia's answers.

They tried in vain to drag the secret from her.

"I'll find out how to do it," the Administrator

concluded when he dismissed her, "even if I have to kill these youngsters."

Meanwhile, Francisco and Jacinta, leaning on the parapet of the well, were crying bitterly. Lúcia went to meet them! What joy!

"Ah! You've come back! Your sister, who came for water, told us that they had killed you. We prayed and wept so much for you."

In Vila Nova de Ourém

Two days later, on 13 August, the Administrator went to see the parish priest of Fatima, and ordered him to send for the three children. The Administrator questioned them in the presence of the people gathered in the market-place, then he made them get into the carriage, telling them that he was taking them to the Cova da Iria.

When they had travelled several kilometres the carriage took a different direction.

"The Cova da Iria is on the other side," the children told him.

"I know that, but first we're going to visit the parish priest of Vila Nova de Ourém who wants to see you and question you. After that, I'll bring you back by car and you'll still arrive in time at the Cova da Iria."

To ride in a car was a great attraction for them. They remained silent. When they reached Vila Nova de Ourém, they insisted on being taken at once to the parish priest. They were told that first they had to have lunch. Thus the time for their meeting with

Our Lady went by. What sorrow for their little hearts! What a satanic joy for the Administrator!

In jail

When they had begun to think that they could go home, the Administrator returned to the fray with his questions. The secret, however, was not revealed.

To be beaten by a child is the last straw for a proud man. So the Administrator had recourse to his authority. He arrested the three little shepherds. He ordered them to be locked in a room, saying that they would not get out unless they first told him the secret. They remained there all night. Early next morning, an old woman tried to drag the secret from them, but in vain. Then they were taken to the Administrator, who threatened, questioned, made promises of shining gold coins; but nothing could shake the determination of those little confidants of Our Lady.

In the afternoon, they were taken to the public jail and told they would be collected later – to be burnt alive; but they still did not speak and revealed absolutely nothing.

In jail! Three innocent children among thieves, blasphemers, wretched criminals!

What affected Jacinta most was not the place or the company, but the thought of her mother so far away. She went to the window, away from her companions, where she cried bitterly.

"Jacinta!" called Lúcia, "Come here – why are you crying?"

"Because we're going to die without ever seeing our parents. Nobody will come to see us. I want at least to see my mother!"

"Don't cry," Francisco encouraged her. "If we can never see our mother again, it can't be helped! We'll offer this sacrifice for the conversion of sinners. It would be worse if Our Lady never came back. That's what I would mind most. But I'm offering that too for sinners."

Joining his hands he made his offering.

"Oh my Jesus, it is for love of you and for the conversion of sinners."

"And also for the Holy Father and in reparation for offences committed against the Immaculate Heart of Mary," added Jacinta, with tears in her eyes.

The others prisoners, touched, wanted to console them.

"Why don't you tell the Administrator the secret? What does it matter to you that the Lady doesn't want that?"

"Never!" Jacinta answered vehemently. "I'd rather die!"

That particular day, they hadn't said the Rosary. They looked around ... no picture on the wall. Jacinta improvised an altar. She took out a medallion, asked one of the prisoners to hang it on the wall and, with the other two, knelt down to pray. The other prisoners were drawn to imitate this gesture, and the Hail Mary's of the little shepherds mingled with those of people who had not prayed, perhaps, for a very long time.

Some hours later, the Administrator sent for them again in his office. Questions and threats yielded no better results this time.

"If you don't want to obey willingly, you'll obey unwillingly!" shouted the infuriated Administrator, jumping to his feet.

He called a guard and ordered him, in a loud voice – so that the children would hear – to prepare a big cauldron of boiling oil in which to burn the little rebels, who were meanwhile locked in a nearby room. They were left there for a while in frightened suspense. When the door opened again, one name was heard, the name of the smallest. It was the Administrator, in another attempt to make them talk.

"If you refuse to speak, you will be the first to be burned," he said. "Come with me."

Jacinta didn't cry. She thought joyfully that soon she would go to join her beautiful Lady for ever.

The Administrator caressed her, questioned her and threatened her, all to no avail. He then sent her to a room in a distant part of the house.

Francisco is put to the test

Meanwhile, Francisco said to Lúcia:

"If they kill us, as they say they will, we'll soon be in heaven. I don't really mind dying."

But he was thinking of Jacinta, who might possibly have a moment of weakness, and he thought it was his duty to help her. "God grant that Jacinta is not afraid," he said. "I'm going to say a Hail Mary for her."

He was still praying, bareheaded, when the door opened again.

"That girl is already dead. Now it's your turn!" shouted the Administrator, making for Francisco, who remained quite calm. "Out with the secret!"

"I can't tell it to anyone."

"You can't? We'll see about that! Come on!" And seizing him by the arm, he dragged Francisco with him.

The result of this interrogation was no more satisfying for the Administrator than the previous one. Francisco was locked in a room where he met his sister. What delight for their little hearts!

Only Lúcia remained. She was convinced that the Administrator had meant what he said, but she wasn't afraid. She was praying to Our Lady for courage, and Our Lady did not let her down. Thus, Lúcia also was sent to join her cousins.

On the following day, 15 August, there was one last attempt to make them talk. Since the children emerged victorious, the Administrator was obliged to take them home to Fatima, from where he had deceitfully taken them two days before.

An unexpected visit

Glad in one respect that they had been victorious, the three were sorrowful at the same time, because of their unavoidable failure to appear at the holm-oak on the 13th. Would Our Lady forgive them? It wasn't their fault.

Six days after the meeting they had missed, they

were grazing the flock at a place called Valinhos. At the usual time for the apparitions, the familiar signs appeared in the sky. Oh! How their hearts beat for joy! Once again, they were immersed in that sweet ecstasy, in conversation with the lovely Lady.

She spoke to them, deploring the fact that they had been prevented from going to the Cova da Iria, and told them that because of this, the miracle promised for October would be less impressive. She again urged them to say the Rosary every day for the peace of the world, answered Lúcia's questions and concluded:

"Pray, pray very much for sinners. Many, many souls go to hell because there is no one to make sacrifices and pray for them."

Having given her message for the month of August, she disappeared.

Before this, the children had been distressed to see the holm-oak at the Cova da Iria stripped of its leaves by the people's piety. This time, however, they cut off the branch on which Our Lady's feet had rested and carried it home triumphantly.

"Aunt," shouted Jacinta, "we saw Our Lady again."

"You never do anything but see Our Lady! Liars, all of you!"

"Yes, Aunt! It's true! Look: she had one foot on this branch and the other on that one."

Her aunt took the branch in her hand, seeing the leaves folded almost at a right angle. She and others present all perceived a sweet perfume. She was impressed and recognised this as a sign that not everything Lúcia said was a lie. Thus, the little girl's life became easier and some measure of peace returned to the home.

The external difficulties increased, but the children's courage increased in proportion.

One day, three people with rather unfriendly faces, after a long cross-examination, concluded:

"If you don't make up your minds to tell the secret, the Administrator will order you to be killed."

"That's wonderful!" Jacinta exclaimed joyfully. "I love Jesus and Our Lady so much! In that way we'll go to join them more quickly."

Talking among themselves, they consoled one another:

"If they kill us, all the better; we'll go to heaven all the quicker."

It is always true that the Lord "never allows us to be tried beyond our strength".

The last apparitions

The September apparition took place. The three children had their interview with the lovely Lady, who for the fifth time told them to say the Rosary every day. She promised to return in October, along with St Joseph and the Child Jesus. The little shepherds never doubted the fidelity of the heavenly Vision (had they not experienced it several times?). They waited confidently. This would be the last apparition, the one in which the crowd would see an impressive miracle.

In Aljustrel there was great excitement. People were afraid that the civil authorities would plant a bomb beside the little seers at the moment of the apparition, but they themselves were not afraid.

"Wouldn't it be marvellous," they exclaimed, "if we could go straight up to heaven with Our Lady!"

A distinguished lady (a great friend of Jacinta and Francisco) warned them:

"Children, if the miracle you have announced does not take place, God help you! These people are capable of burning you alive!"

"We're not afraid," they declared with a smile, "because Our Lady does not deceive us. She told us there will be a great miracle and that all will see it."

The parents of the little shepherds were excited too. Lúcia's mother was in a continual state of perplexity. She wanted to believe all that her daughter had said, and yet she feared that she might have been the victim of a hoax. Very worried, on the morning of the 12th, the day before the great event, she woke Lúcia very early.

"Come, daughter," she told her, "we'd better go to Confession. There are people saying that we're all going to die tomorrow at the Cova da Iria. If Our Lady doesn't work the miracle, people will kill us. So it's better for us to go to Confession so as to be better prepared."

"Mother, go to Confession if you want to," Lúcia answered calmly, "I'll go with you, but not because of what they are saying. I'm not afraid to die. I'm absolutely certain that Our Lady will do as she promised."

After the conversation, Lúcia's mother didn't think any more about going to Confession because of the miracle.

13 October

The 13th of October dawned, dull and cold. The Cova da Iria was swarming with people. Pilgrims and onlookers were drenched to the skin. What did it matter, if soon they were to see something extraordinary?

Just before midday, the children arrived, dressed in their Sunday clothes and carrying bunches of flowers.

There were seventy thousand spectators, all crowding to get near the children.

Poor little ones!

Jacinta was exhausted.

"Don't push me!" she begged, in tears.

Some men offered to protect her. Francisco and Lúcia placed themselves among them. At a certain moment, Lúcia told everyone to close their umbrellas. It was pouring with rain. Nevertheless, no one offered any resistance. All recited the Rosary aloud and the echo resounded: once ... twice ... three times ... all the different voices.

Midday – the time of the apparitions; a flash, a moment of expectation for all. Then:

"Here she is, here she is," cried Lúcia, "I see her."

Her mother, who was beside her, didn't see anything. She was afraid and murmured in her distress:

"Look carefully, child: make sure you are not mistaken."

But Lúcia didn't hear her. She was in ecstasy: her face assumed a rosy hue; her full lips were finer. She was beautiful, very beautiful.

Francisco and Jacinta were also in ecstasy before the beautiful Vision and felt they were in Paradise.

The crowd waited anxiously, in suspense... Around the little shepherds who had moved to the site of the Apparitions (marked by two lighted lamps hanging from a kind of arch made by sticks) the pilgrims noticed – three times – the formation of a little cloud which rose towards the sky. But they didn't see anything except the movement of Lúcia's lips as she asked:

"Who are you and what do you want of us?"

"I am the Lady of the Rosary," Our Lady replied graciously. "I have come to warn people to change their lives and not to offend Our Lord any more by sin, for he is already deeply offended, and to tell them to say the Rosary every day to obtain peace for the world. They must also do penance for their own sins." She continued: "I want a chapel in my honour to be built here, in this place."

She assured them that the war would soon end and that she would hear their prayers. She saluted them with motherly kindness. She opened her radiant hands, pointed to the sun and disappeared.

"Look at the sun!" shouted Lúcia, hardly aware of what she was saying.

A shiver ran through the huge crowd, waiting expectantly. The rain stopped as if by magic; the sun appeared like a great silver moon. It revolved on itself like a Catherine wheel, throwing out great beams of fire. Suddenly it appeared to drop out of the firmament and hurl itself on the crowd. Shouts, terror, professions of faith, fervent prayers. Many, kneeling on the muddy ground, were beating their breasts.

"A miracle!" Clothes, drenched with rain, were now discovered to be completely dry.

The prodigy was seen by people thirty or forty kilometres away.

The seventy thousand pilgrims returned home, deeply moved and full of enthusiasm. Our Lady had not disappointed them.

Lúcia, with her mother (now convinced), returned to her own house, which was relatively more modest than that of her cousins.

Francisco and Jacinta returned home too. All three were thinking nostalgically of the beautiful Lady who lived for ever in their simple, pure hearts, but who would never more come to them at the Cova of the miracle.

Heroic sufferings

While Fatima, along with the world of Catholics and Freemasons alike, was pronouncing judgement on these extraordinary facts, the three children continued to mind their sheep and live their lives as usual.

Francisco always wanted to console the Lord, Lúcia was always generous. Jacinta, the smallest of them, was always careful not to miss a single opportunity for sacrifice.

"Francisco," Lúcia asked him one day, "what do you like best: consoling Our Lord or converting sinners so that no more souls will go to hell?"

"I'd rather console Our Lord. Didn't you notice that Our Lady became sad when she was telling us not to offend Our Lord any more because he was already so much offended? I love Our Lord so much! But he is so sad because of all the sins! We won't ever commit another sin," he repeated. And he offered his prayers and fasts for this intention.

The others also learned to fast.

When they were thirsty they learned to deny themselves to the point of heroism.

It was the height of summer. Early one morning they took the flock to a place some distance away. Their parents had told them not to return until night for fear of sunstroke and so they were given their dinner to take with them. On the way, they met their little 'friends'. Jacinta, always so generous, joyfully gave them not only their lunch but their dinner too, leaving nothing for themselves.

Towards midday, the blazing sun seemed to be burning up the land around them. Even more than hunger, the children were suffering the torments of thirst. They offered it up as a sacrifice several times. But at length they could hold out no longer. They went to a neighbouring house to ask for water. A kind old woman gave them some bread, which they divided between them, and a jug of water, which Lúcia gave to Francisco.

"Drink some!"

"I don't want to drink."

"Why?"

"So as to suffer for the conversion of sinners."

"Jacinta, you drink some."

"I want to make a sacrifice too, for sinners."

Lúcia (who also made the sacrifice) with great satisfaction poured the water into a cavity in a rock so that the sheep could drink, and then ran off, jubilant, to return the jug.

But the suffocating heat showed no sign of growing less and the hours seemed interminable; the croaking of the frogs and the chirping of the cicadas seemed to increase the heat of the atmosphere to the point of being almost unbearable. The crickets joined in the deafening noise.

Little Jacinta, worn out with hunger and thirst, could not endure it any longer. Turning to Lúcia, she said:

"Go and tell the cicadas and the ants to keep quiet. They give me a headache. I can't bear it any more!"

"What? You don't want to offer this sacrifice for sinners?" Lúcia observed.

"Yes! I do! Let them chirp on."

They had learnt to put up with thirst and they managed to spend the whole suffocating month of August without drinking a single drop of water!

What heroism! The discovery of another sacrifice was a brilliant idea.

One afternoon, they were amusing themselves by gathering flowers. Jacinta inadvertently touched a nettle.

"Look, look!" she said triumphantly to the other two, clasping in her hands the pungent leaves. "Another way to make sacrifices."

From time to time the three children would beat their legs with nettles, never telling anyone about this or the other sacrifices. Thus no one knew about the rope.

One day (it was the end of August) when they were going up the hill, they found a rope on the road. Lúcia, as if she were playing, tied it around her arm.

"Do you know what?" she said triumphantly "This is painful! We could tie it around our waists and offer the sacrifice to Our Lord!"

Our Lady had asked them several times to offer sacrifices for sinners. The three were very pleased with this discovery. But there was only one rope. Who was to have it? All three wanted it. What could be done? With a sharp stone they divided it into three. They tied it round their waists, next to the skin. Rough as it was, it must have caused them much discomfort, so much so that Jacinta, who used to tighten it in order to suffer more, could often not restrain her tears.

"Take it off," the other two would tell her, but nevertheless, they continued to wear theirs.

"Oh no!" the little one would reply. "I want to

offer this sacrifice to Our Lord to make reparation to him for the insults he receives and for the conversion of sinners."

Therefore happily she kept it on.

At first they wore it, like a real hair shirt, day and night. Their health began to deteriorate. But what did they know about that, thirsting as they were for penance? And how could other people know about it, if they themselves had jealously hidden all their acts of self-denial?

However, Our Lady knew about it, and in the apparition of the following month (13 September), among other things, she said to them with motherly kindness:

"Our Lord is very pleased with your sacrifices; but he doesn't want you to sleep with the rope. Wear it during the day only."

They obeyed. Francisco and Jacinta did not leave it off even in their last illness. It was, in fact, stained with their blood.

Jacinta was right when, childlike, she confided to the other two:

"Our Lord must be very pleased with our sacrifices!"

Amidst the fragrance of violets

In order that these sacrifices, mystical flowers whose corollas shed their perfume eternally in heaven, may be really worthy of a reward, they have to grow amidst the fragrance of violets. Humility must precede, accompany and follow every act of virtue, unless we want even our best actions to be for ever wasted.

Who taught these children that?

Nobody, or better, God himself, through the contact with Our Lady.

In their angelic simplicity, they discovered how to run away from constant praise, from signs of veneration. The more they were sought the more they hid themselves. So many people were looking for them!

One day they were sitting at the door of their home when they saw some people coming towards them. Lúcia and Francisco ran to the bedroom to hide under the bed, but not Jacinta.

"I didn't hide," she said. "I offered the sacrifice to Our Lord."

The people went up to her, waited a while and finally decided to go away. When the other two came out of their hiding-place, they asked Jacinta:

"What did you say when they asked you about us?"

"Nothing! I put my head down. I just kept my eyes on the ground and said nothing. I always do that when I can't tell the truth. I don't want to tell lies because that's a sin."

Another time, they heard that some people were looking for them. Francisco ran to the others who were sitting in the shade of a big fig tree.

"Let's cover ourselves with these hats," he said. "We can climb up the tree, and with our heads hidden they won't see us."

The gentlemen passed by without seeing them. The children, delighted with the success of their ruse, came down and went to hide in the middle of the wheat.

On another occasion, they saw on the road a large motor car from which some elegantly dressed ladies and gentlemen alighted.

"Would they have come to see us?"

"Let's run away!"

"Impossible, they'd see us. Better stay where we are. They won't know us."

They walked a bit faster. The strangers stopped them and asked:

"Are you from Aljustrel?"

"Yes, we are, sir."

"Do you know the three little shepherds to whom Our Lady appeared?"

"We do, sir."

"Could you tell us where they live?"

"Yes. Continue along that road. Down there, turn right, then left…"

They described in minute detail the way to their own houses.

"We should always do that!" little Jacinta said with satisfaction.

"Why did you always hide yourselves?" Lúcia was once asked when she had become a nun.

"Because", she answered simply, "so much praise embarrassed us."

Sometimes, when Lúcia was minding the flock, her cousins had to leave her in order to be available to visitors, but they couldn't be found anywhere.

Where did they hide for hours on end? Nobody ever knew, except Lúcia, who eventually told us that they used to go to the cave in the hill where they spent hours saying the Rosary and making sacrifices known only to Our Lord.

When they were attending the school in Fatima, they took advantage of the proximity of a church in order to visit the 'Hidden Jesus'. But the Lord knew how to ask them for further sacrifices. Hardly had they entered the church when they were surrounded by people asking for prayers and telling them their troubles.

"It seemed as if they guessed – they never left us in peace with Jesus."

But, when it was a question of praying for some sinner, all their sacrifices seemed few.

"Let's pray, let's pray," they would say, "we'll offer a whole lot of sacrifices to Our Lord so that he will be converted, poor man!"

Away by himself

One afternoon, Francisco's mother was rather anxious. He had disappeared some hours before and nobody knew anything about it.

When Lúcia and Jacinta arrived, his mother asked them to go and look for him.

Where would they find him? In the cave on the hill? They sat down whilst they discussed whether to go there to look for him. In the meantime Francisco's mother left the house.

"Jacinta, Lúcia, here I am!" It was Francisco's voice: he was in the loft.

"What are you doing up there?" they asked him, surprised and laughing.

"Eh! There were so many people," he explained, while coming down, "I didn't want them to meet me while I was alone. What could I say to them?"

There were days when none of them could be found. Where did they hide? Not down at the end of Lúcia's garden – they could easily be found there – but in a cave nearby, very, very dark, hidden in the thickets. They used to spend hours on end there saying the Rosary, repeating the Angel's prayer, prostrate on the ground as on that first occasion. Francisco, however, could not bear lying prostrate for hours and he was always the first to get up; he would then kneel or sit until the other two were finished.

"I'm not able to stay like that as long as you two," he would say, "it hurts my back so much that I can't bear it any longer."

Sincerity

Francisco was incapable of telling a lie, because lying, as well as offending Our Lord, was naturally repugnant to him, and was therefore to be avoided at all costs.

"If it were a lie," he said once, "it could not be said."

Francisco was loyal and straightforward in all circumstances. One day when he was present, Lúcia was asked whether Our Lady had asked them to pray for sinners.

"No," she answered.

Francisco thought that his cousin was not telling the truth. Soon afterwards, he called her aside to tell her gently, but as if his heart was broken:

"Lúcia, you told a lie. Why did you say that Our Lady didn't tell us to pray for sinners?"

"If you remember," Lúcia answered, smiling at her little cousin's anxiety, "Our Lady told us to pray for peace, so that the war would end. As for sinners, she only told us to make sacrifices."

"Ah! You're right!" he agreed, hitting his forehead with his hand, as if to say "How forgetful I am!"

Thus, with an act of humility, he confirmed his devotion to the truth.

Somebody wanted him to graze their flock beside his godmother's meadow. She was so fond of him that she certainly would not have minded. But Francisco simply could not take the flock there. He was afraid it would be stealing. He only took the sheep there when his godmother herself had assured him that she would be pleased if he did.

Sincerity always leads to justice, even in the smallest things. It is true, however, that once, he yielded to the temptation of stealing a few escudos from his father to buy a harmonica. But he repented, accused himself of it and confessed it several times.

Wouldn't it be good, if some boys who have no scruples about stealing money from their parents would only imitate him!

Charity

Francisco, whose tender heart was so moved by the sufferings of Jesus, would not have been genuine if he had not sought to open it to others also. For him, helping others was a need. Have we not seen him giving away his lunch on more than one occasion?

In the village there was one of those old women whom everybody calls 'aunt': in this case, 'Aunt Maria'. A semi-invalid, she found it very difficult to gather her flock of goats and sheep: the animals used to run away from her, to the left and to the right, but when she saw Francisco, the poor old lady stopped worrying. In fact, he ran like a squirrel to help her and didn't even want her to thank him.

I wonder if there are some people who perform little acts of kindness only in the hope of a reward?

His extraordinary sensitiveness

Extremely sensitive, Francisco couldn't bear to look at people who were deformed, or in any way unfortunate.

"It makes me so sad," he would say woefully.

If he was asked to visit somebody he didn't know, he would first find out if the person was ill. If that was the case he felt obliged to refuse.

"I can't," he would say, "tell him I will pray for him."

Once he was invited into a house. The mother and her son were deaf-mutes. Francisco excused himself saying:

"These people who want to talk and cannot, make me so sad. I pray for them."

On another occasion, Francisco was on his way to the Cova along with Lúcia and Jacinta. Along the road, they were surprised by some people who were waiting for them. In order to see and hear them more easily, they put the two girls on top of a little wall. Francisco, always fond of hiding, ran away and hid behind a wall where he found the opportunity to practise charity.

There was a poor woman and a boy with her who had both been longing to talk alone with the little seers. The moment was just right. Kneeling down, Francisco gave them an invitation:

"Would you like to say the Rosary with me?"

Later, the woman, together with her husband and her son, were seen praying at the spot of the apparitions, thanking Our Lady for the favours they had received.

With the Hidden Jesus

A young man from a neighbouring village was arrested, though innocent, and would incur a serious penalty if he could not prove his innocence. This would not be easy to do, and so his family asked Lúcia to pray for him.

At that time a school for girls had opened in Fatima. Jacinta and Lúcia attended it, and used to walk there accompanied by Francisco who was on his way to the boys' school. As they walked, Lúcia told her cousins about the sad case of the young man. They would have to pray hard for him. When they arrived in Fatima, Francisco suggested:

"Look. This is what we'll do. You two go on to school and I'll stay in the church keeping Jesus company and praying for this intention."

They did so.

When school was over, Lúcia went to him:

"Did you ask for that favour, Francisco?"

"I did. Tell him he'll be home in a few days."

And that's exactly what happened.

Another time, Francisco remained alone with some visitors who had come to see him. Jacinta and Lúcia ran away and hid. When the visitors departed, the two girls came to Francisco and asked him how he had managed, to which he replied:

"There were many people. They wanted to know where you two were, but I didn't know. There was a lady who wanted the cure of a sick person and the conversion of a sinner. I'll pray for that. You two can pray for the others, there were so many of them."

This time, as on many other occasions, Our Lady heard the prayers of her little shepherds.

The prayers of good children are always heard, in one way or another.

For the Holy Father

The Holy Father? Our Lady spoke of him, but Jacinta didn't know who he was.

One day, among the many visitors, there were two priests. As they were leaving, they asked the children to pray for the Holy Father. In reply to

Jacinta's question, they explained who he was and why he needed prayers so much. Jacinta was so consumed with love that, every time she offered a sacrifice to Jesus, she never failed to add, "and for the Holy Father".

All three learned the lovely custom of saying three Hail Mary's at the end of the Rosary for the Holy Father.

Jacinta used to say often:

"How I would love to see the Holy Father! So many people come here but the Holy Father never comes."

One day the parish priest said that Lúcia would probably have to go to Rome to be questioned. When she told her cousins this, they replied with tears in their eyes:

"Lucky you! We'll never go there. But we're offering this sacrifice for the Pope."

How many sacrifices did Jacinta add to that one! She would say, alluding to the secret confided to them by Our Lady:

"Poor Holy Father! I'm so sorry for him."

One day when they were on their knees, reciting the Angel's prayer, Jacinta stood up and said to Lúcia:

"Look! Don't you see all those roads and fields full of people crying with hunger and with nothing to eat? And the Holy Father praying in front of the Immaculate Heart of Mary!"

Another priest suggested to the children some short prayers with which they could enrich their days.

Jacinta particularly liked these two: 'My Jesus, I love you' and 'Sweet Heart of Mary, be my salvation'.

From another short prayer they learned to thank the Lord for the graces they had received.

Jacinta, always so fervent, even in the liveliest part of a game, would ask:

"Did you remember to tell Our Lord that you love him because of all the graces he has given you?"

For herself, she would repeat often:

"I love Our Lord and Our Lady so much and I never get tired of telling them that I love them."

As the days passed, her love grew. She confided to Lúcia:

"I just love telling Jesus that I love him. When I say that a good many times I seem to have a fire in my breast, but a fire that won't burn me." On another occasion she said, "If only I could make everybody's heart burn with the fire that I feel in here, how wonderful it would be!"

The time was approaching for her to fulfil her desire: from her place in heaven, to make the Immaculate Heart of Mary and the Sacred Heart of Jesus loved.

Chapter 6

Like a burning lamp

Francisco had to change his way of life in some ways now that he was going to school.

He had not been minding the flock for some time now because his mother felt she had to sell it since the children had to be constantly available to the pilgrims.

He was not however as enthusiastic as the other boys were about going to school.

"What's the sense of going to school?" he would say. "I'm going to heaven soon."

But he enjoyed the walk from home to school because it gave him the opportunity to sometimes visit the parish church where he could meet the 'Hidden Jesus'. Francisco learned how to listen to him, even without seeing him.

Often, he simply couldn't leave that little bit of heaven, beside the Tabernacle, and he would say to Lúcia:

"Listen, you go on to school, I'm going to stay here with Jesus. Come back on your way home."

But when Lúcia returned, it always seemed to him that the time had simply flown. He hungered for Jesus and nourished himself by means of constant prayer.

A priest had taught the three of them some short prayers: "My Jesus, I love you", "Sweet Heart of Mary, be my salvation", and Francisco used to repeat these prayers innumerable times a day.

Another priest had taught him to thank Our Lord like this:

"My God, I love you, in thanksgiving for the favours you have given me."

Francisco, like Jacinta and Lúcia, was a lamp continually burning which enlightened all who came near it.

"We don't know what it is about Francisco," all those who knew him used to say, "but when we are with him we all feel better."

They were influenced, certainly, by his virtue, his love for Our Lord and Our Lady. He aroused this love in others in ways that were imperceptible. Thus he carried out the task which had been given him.

I can't give a blessing

Francisco, always docile and gracious, became strong and decisive when it was a question of preventing harm.

One day, on his way home, he met a lady accompanied by a good number of people. She was a fraud who pretended to bless religious objects with a view to making money. When the little shepherd came closer she invited him to bless something, but he remained calm and said:

"I can't give a blessing and neither can you. Only priests can do that."

Soon afterwards, Francisco's words passed from mouth to mouth, and the woman left the village at once because of the threats of those who had been deceived by her.

One day, during his illness, he gently scolded Lúcia, saying:

"Why do you go around with all those girls? Don't go around with them any more. When you come out of school, here's the best thing to do: go into the church for a moment to make a visit to Jesus, and then go home quickly."

Lúcia, although she was older, valued this wise and prudent advice.

"Jesus is not pleased"

Francisco tried all the time to be better, so as to be ready for heaven, especially after the apparitions. Lúcia was still slightly frivolous and vain, and Francisco let her see that this was not fitting. He also scolded Jacinta because of her craze for dancing.

One Sunday afternoon, when they walked by Lúcia's godmother's house, they were invited in.

"It's so long since I saw you!" the lady said, making a great fuss of them.

Three more children arrived, having noticed the presence of the little shepherds. Soon, there was a considerable gathering.

It should be noted that Jacinta was really mad

about dancing, having seen it so many times in houses and yards. She only needed to hear an instrument in order to start dancing with friends or by herself, just as she had seen people do so often. Lúcia also, though less fascinated, danced willingly when she could.

Delighted with the little party, the godmother invited the children to dance and sing. They knew a great many songs. The party was lively. Other neighbours arrived. But Francisco was annoyed. Jesus was sad and this was the way they were consoling him? He went over to Lúcia.

"Listen," he said, "we mustn't sing these songs. Jesus is certainly not pleased."

And they left the party to make reparation with a prayer beside the well, which had become their favourite spot.

Another time, Francisco intervened in a similar way.

Lúcia and Jacinta had allowed themselves to be persuaded to take part in a dance. This time, Francisco simply could not understand the girls' conduct. In Jacinta's case it wasn't so bad since she was so young, but Lúcia... And so, not standing on ceremony, he scolded her:

"You, Lúcia, are you going back to those foolish amusements? Have you forgotten that you promised Our Lord to give them up?"

"I didn't want to go," his cousin answered, ashamed, "but they won't leave us alone, and I don't know how I'm going to get out of it."

"Do you know what you should do?" Francisco

suggested. "They all know that you saw Our Lady. Tell them that you promised not to dance any more and so you're not going to."

The 'Hidden Jesus' gave Francisco true wisdom. The little boy made it his own and passed it on to others.

The little schoolboy from Aljustrel became the interpreter of the Divine Master's wishes.

Chapter 7
The road to Calvary

The war was over. In many homes there was no one to answer when the children called for their daddy; when wives sought in vain the earthly support of their inseparable companion; when mothers could only cherish sorrowfully in their hearts the face of a son who would never return. Bullets had killed many young men. Now, instead, there arrived a terrible bronchopneumonia called 'Spanish influenza', which claimed an incalculable number of victims all over Europe.

On 23 December 1918, Jacinta and Francisco also fell ill.

Francisco prepared himself with ardour because he knew he was going to die soon. Our Lady had told him so when she said that he had to say many Rosaries. And the little shepherd indeed said many.

Jacinta was happy to suffer because, in this way, "the Lord will convert many sinners".

Just as when they were well, they started a competition to see who could make the most sacrifices.

"How many sacrifices did you give Our Lord last night?" Francisco asked in the morning.

"I got up three times to say the Angel's prayer."

"I", Francisco said, "made so many that it is impossible to count them. I had a lot of pain and I didn't complain."

They loved to be with Lúcia who came very often to see them. But they knew how to give that up generously too. If she visited Jacinta first, the little girl would ask her gently:

"Now go and see Francisco: I'll make the sacrifice of being alone."

"Do you know what?" she confided one day. "My mother went out and I wanted to go and talk to Francisco, but I didn't go."

Another time she made this admission:

"My head hurts me a lot, and I'm very thirsty, but I don't want to drink anything so as to suffer more for sinners."

"Tell Jesus that I send him all my love," she asked Lúcia when she called in on her way to school.

Oh! How little Jacinta always loved her 'Hidden Jesus'.

One day she declared to Lúcia:

"It won't be long before I go to heaven. You will stay longer here on earth, to tell everyone that Our Lord wants to establish in the world devotion to the Immaculate Heart of Mary. When you have to talk about that, don't hide away. Tell everybody that God grants his graces through the Immaculate Heart of Mary. Let them ask her: let them honour her along with the Sacred Heart of Jesus."

At other times, however, her childish vivacity

made Jacinta forget her interior commitment. Thus, one day, she refused to take a little milk, in spite of the loving insistence of her mother.

"Is that the way you obey your mother?" Lúcia asked as soon as they were alone. "Why don't you offer that sacrifice to Our Lord?"

With tears in her eyes, the little girl confessed that she hadn't thought of that and called her mother. She asked forgiveness and swallowed the milk.

"If you only knew how much that cost me, Lúcia! Every day that goes by," she added, "I feel a greater distaste for milk and for soup; but I don't say anything and I take everything for love of Our Lord and the Immaculate Heart of Mary."

"How are you?" Lúcia asked her one day.

"You know I'll never get better. I have had pains in my chest. But I don't say anything and I suffer for the conversion of sinners."

Sometimes Lúcia, knowing how Jacinta loved flowers, used to take her lilies and begonias.

"Take them," she would say to Jacinta, "they're from the Cabeço."

Jacinta would thank her and, with a heart full of sadness, would say:

"I'll never go back there again."

"But what difference does it make, if you're going to see Our Lady and Our Lord?"

"That's true," Jacinta would answer happily.

And she would pick the petals off the flowers, counting them as she did so.

A few days after she had fallen out of bed she

gave Lúcia her piece of rope. It had three knots and was bloodstained.

"Take it," she said, "and keep it, because I'm afraid my mother will see it. But if I get better I'll want it again."

At the Cova da Iria

Francisco had to say many Rosaries and he had already said many. Now, however, his weakness was such that he couldn't manage a whole Rosary. "Mother," he would say regretfully, "I'm not able to say the Rosary. When I get to the end, I just can't do any more."

"Pray it in your head if you can't say the words," his mother told him. "Our Lady looks at your heart and she'll be just as pleased."

But he suffered because he thought he couldn't pray properly like the others.

He was told to take little walks in the fresh air. Gathering all his strength, he went a few times to the Cova da Iria. There he would pray and gaze at that part of the sky from where Our Lady had come and where she had gone up again. Oh, soon he would be with her!

Some people told him he was going to get better, but he had no illusions. In any case, he wasn't worried about it – on the contrary. Once, his godmother, in his presence, promised to offer Our Lady as many kilos of wheat as Francisco weighed. He smiled and answered that the promise was quite useless. He would never get better.

In bed again

At the end of February 1919, Francisco began to get visibly worse and had to take to his bed again. Jacinta kept him company.

One morning they asked their sister, Teresa, to go and call Lúcia at once.

What had happened?

Our Lady! Our Lady had come to visit Francisco and told him that she would soon come for him. As for Jacinta, she still had much to suffer. And she said she was ready for that: to suffer for sinners, for the Holy Father and for the triumph of the Immaculate Heart of Mary.

Francisco gave his approval. He would suffer also for the same intentions.

One day, Francisco said to Lúcia and Jacinta who had gone to visit him:

"Don't talk much today because my head is hurting me."

"Don't forget to offer your sufferings for sinners," Jacinta suggested,

"Yes, but first I offer them to console Our Lord and Our Lady; only after that for sinners and for the Holy Father."

In the last days of March he became worse.

"Look, Lúcia," he said, "I'm very ill. It won't be long now before I go to heaven."

"Listen, then, to what I'm going to say to you," said Lúcia. "Don't forget to pray hard, up there in heaven, for sinners and for the Holy Father, for Jacinta and for me."

"Yes. I'll pray. But you had better recommend

those intentions to Jacinta, because I'm afraid that I'll forget all that when I see Our Lord."

He was always true to himself, the little boy who was afraid to promise anything he couldn't be absolutely certain of carrying out.

On 2 April, his condition worsened. He hadn't yet made his First Communion, and he complained about this to his mother.

Meanwhile they sent for the priest.

Francisco sent at once for Lúcia who arrived in the twinkling of an eye.

"Lúcia," he said, "I want to go to Confession so as to be able to receive my First Communion before I die. Tell me if you ever saw me commit a sin."

"A few times," she answered after a moment's thought. "You disobeyed your mother when she told you to stay in the house, and you came to talk to me."

"That's true, thank you! Now, go and ask Jacinta if she remembers any others."

Jacinta remembered that one day, before the apparitions, he had secretly taken some money from his father to buy a harmonica and that, along with other boys, he had thrown stones at the boys from Boleiras.

"These", the sick boy said, "I've already confessed, but I'll confess them again. Perhaps, because of those sins, I made Our Lord sad! But even if I don't die, I'll never commit them again. I'm sorry for all the harm I did."

That he had indeed repented was revealed by his attitude as he prayed aloud:

"Oh my Jesus, forgive me my sins, save me from the fires of hell. Lead all souls to heaven, especially those in most need of your mercy."

Then he turned to Lúcia, requesting her also to ask pardon from Our Lord for him.

"I will," his cousin answered, "but Our Lord has already pardoned you since the moment Our Lady said she would soon come to bring you to heaven with her. Now, I'm going to Mass and I'll pray to the 'Hidden Jesus' for you."

"Listen," he begged once more, "ask the parish priest to bring me Holy Communion."

That was his last request.

When Lúcia came back and told him that she had prayed for him, his painfully thin little face lit up and he smiled as he promised her:

"In heaven I'll pray for you. You are staying down here because that's what Our Lady wants. So try and do everything she tells you."

Later, when the parish priest arrived, he heard Francisco's confession and promised to bring him Holy Communion the following day.

Francisco was happy. To those who came to see him, he announced joyfully:

"Tomorrow morning, I'm going to receive the 'Hidden Jesus'… Tomorrow the parish priest is bringing me Holy Communion."

He continued fasting. When, at last, the longed-for time came, Francisco wanted to sit up in bed, so as to receive Holy Communion more reverently, but, because of his extreme weakness, was not allowed. A precious sacrifice to add to all the others!

With Jesus at last

When the parish priest placed the Sacred Host on Francisco's bloodless lips, he tasted to the full the sweetness of his Lord's presence.

Now the Lord was not hidden before Francisco, but Francisco was hidden in Jesus and the two were one.

Who could imagine the exchanges during those moments? Francisco was happy!

"Mother," he asked when he came out of his ecstasy, "can't I receive Our Lord again?"

And to Jacinta:

"Today I'm more fortunate than you, because I have in my heart the 'Hidden Jesus'."

Later, he asked pardon of his parents, his brothers, sisters and his godmother. He asked Lúcia and Jacinta to say the Rosary for him since he hadn't the strength to do so himself and he would follow it in his thoughts and in his heart.

"...Pray for us sinners, now and at the hour of our death."

"Are you suffering much, Francisco?" they asked at the end of the Rosary.

"A good bit, but it doesn't matter. I'm suffering for Jesus, and besides, I'm soon going to heaven."

He looked at Jacinta. Within a short time they would be together for ever in Paradise.

Then he looked at Lúcia. He had loved her very much on earth. How would he do without her in heaven? He could not help saying to her:

"For sure, in heaven, I'll miss you very much.

Oh! If only Our Lady would send for you to go there quickly!"

The last farewell

It was very late that night when Lúcia took leave of Francisco, bidding him farewell:

"Goodbye, Francisco! If you go to heaven tonight, don't forget me up there."

"Don't worry. I'll never forget you."

Taking her right hand, he drew it to him. With tears in his eyes, he gazed at her. Was there something he wanted to say to her? Greatly touched, Lúcia asked him if there was. "No!" he answered in a voice that was scarcely audible.

Francisco's mother asked the girls to leave and she remained at the bedside of her dying son.

"Goodbye, then, Francisco! Until we meet in heaven."

Goodbye? No! The little seer knows that they will all meet some day!

"Goodbye, until we meet in heaven!" he answered.

Jacinta had not said goodbye. When she reached the door, she turned round and said:

"Greet Our Lord and Our Lady for me. Tell them I'll suffer all they want of me, for the conversion of sinners."

Francisco smiled. He was thinking that very soon he would see Jesus and Our Lady.

It was true. The dying boy was exhausted. Many people had come to see him and he smiled at them all. He spoke little but somehow he did good to them all.

One day, a poor woman called Mariana had come into his room. She was in tears because her husband had put their son out of the house and the peace of the family was gone.

"Don't worry," Francisco said, "I'll be in heaven soon and when I get there, I'll ask Our Lady at once for that favour."

And he did in fact obtain it.

"It's a mystery," people visiting him would say. "He's a boy just like others. He doesn't say anything. Nevertheless, in his presence, the atmosphere is different. Going into his room is like going into the church."

Francisco lived with Jesus.

His heart was pure and Jesus was very happy to be there.

A light

On the night of 3 April, he was utterly exhausted but serene. Very serene! While his mother kept watch beside him he slept.

Dawn broke on 4 April 1919, a Friday.

"Mother!"

"Do you feel bad, Francisco?"

He didn't answer, just smiled.

"Look, mother, over there beside the door. Such a beautiful light!"

His mother looked, but did not see anything.

Francisco remained in ecstasy for a few more moments. Then, in a weak voice, he said:

"Now... I don't see it!"

He smiled gently. His eyelids, like the curtains on a stage, came down and veiled for ever those eyes which had seen, on earth, heavenly visions.

Francisco, the little shepherd of Fatima, was not quite eleven years old.

Chapter 8
Jacinta's last days

Little Jacinta had lost much of her vivacity. Pensive and sad, she often spent time on her own thinking about Francisco. The memory of the hours spent with him made her suffer intensely. Oh! She would soon be beside him!

Soon after her brother's death, perhaps as a consequence of the weakness left by the 'Spanish influenza', she was found to have a purulent form of pleurisy which caused her great suffering. She was taken to the hospital in Vila Nova de Ourém, but to no purpose. Two months later she returned home, very ill.

"Yes, I'm suffering a lot... and I'm glad to suffer for the love of Jesus and Our Lady! They love those who suffer for the conversion of sinners."

Jacinta was glad to suffer and she suffered in silence. She returned home with a great open wound, the treatment of which caused her dreadful suffering. She said to Lúcia:

"Don't tell anyone that I'm suffering, even my mother, because I don't want her to be upset."

When her mother looked sad, Jacinta tried to console her:

"Don't be upset, mother, I'm going to heaven and I'll pray hard for you there."

"Don't cry, I'm fine," she told her mother another time.

"Thank you. No, I don't need anything else," she replied to someone who asked her if she needed anything more.

She needed a great many things, but she knew how to do without them, heroically. For example, she would say to Lúcia:

"I'm very thirsty, but I don't want to drink. I'm offering this sacrifice to Jesus for sinners."

"Last night, I was in great pain," she confided to Lúcia on another occasion. "I thought I would offer Jesus the sacrifice of not changing my position in the bed, and so I couldn't sleep any more."

In fact, her face was distorted with pain. "When I'm alone," she said, "I get out of bed several times to say the Angel's prayer. But now I can't bend my forehead to the ground because I'm not steady enough. I pray on my knees only."

Her thirst for sacrifice seemed to increase as her suffering became more intense. She felt such distaste for milk that one day her mother brought her a lovely bunch of grapes, saying:

"If you can't take any more milk, leave it alone and eat these grapes."

"No, mother. I don't want the grapes. Take them home and give me the milk instead."

Her mother was delighted, thinking that Jacinta

had regained her appetite. She would not have thought that if she had heard what the little girl told her cousin in confidence:

"Do you know what," she said, when her mother had gone out, "I would love to have eaten those grapes and it cost me a lot to take the milk, but I wanted to offer that sacrifice to Our Lord."

Our Lady, most certainly, was pleased with such generosity. She rewarded Jacinta, appearing to her again several times.

"Our Lady", Jacinta said to Lúcia one day, "told me that I'll be going to a hospital in Lisbon; that I'll never see you or my parents again and that, after suffering very much, I'll die alone... but that I'm not to be afraid, because she herself will come to take me to heaven."

In tears, she embraced her cousin, saying to her:

"Do you understand? I'll never see you again. I'll die alone. Alone!"

Her worst suffering was the thought of that.

Lúcia was surprised to see her on one occasion, with a holy picture in her hands, saying:

"Heavenly Mother, is it possible that I have to die alone?"

"Don't talk like that! Don't think about it," Lúcia advised.

"No. Let me think about it because the more I think, the more I suffer and I want to suffer a great deal..."

A few moments afterwards, she sighed:

"Oh Jesus, now you can convert many sinners because this sacrifice is very big."

She was right.

In hospital

In the middle of January 1920, a specialist went on pilgrimage to Fatima and wanted to meet the two little seers. Seeing Jacinta so ill, he insisted that she should be taken to Lisbon, in the hope of saving her life with an operation. The family were against it, but the kind doctor did not give up... The little girl left home, accompanied by her mother.

Embracing Lúcia, Jacinta begged her:

"Pray hard for me until I go to heaven. Then, I'll pray for you. Don't tell the secret to anyone, even if they want to kill you. Love Jesus and the Immaculate Heart of Mary very much and make many sacrifices for sinners."

That was her last will and testament.

In Lisbon, she was received into the Orphanage of Our Lady of Miracles. She immediately felt at home there. The Mother Superior became her 'godmother' to whom she confided the treasures of her heart; the little orphans, so many little sisters to bring to Jesus.

Jacinta was happy because she was living under the same roof as her 'Hidden Jesus'. She often spoke about him and received him every day in her heart (she must have received him for the first time, privately, at home in May 1918 or 1919). She visited him often in the chapel, talking intimately, heart to heart to her Jesus, who encouraged her to suffer and revealed the secrets of his love to her.

Our Lady came often to visit her. Talking to Our Lady became a habit with her.

She confided to her godmother the favours of the radiant Lady. She once said to her godmother:

"Come later. Just now I'm expecting Our Lady."

"In order to be truly religious," she said one day, "we have to be pure in soul and body."

"And you know what it is to be pure?"

"I do, yes. To be pure in body is to observe chastity; to be pure in soul is not to commit sins, not to look where we shouldn't, not to steal, not to tell lies but to tell the truth always, even if it costs."

"But who taught you so many things?"

"Our Lady. Some of them, however, I thought of myself. I love to think."

Prophecies fulfilled

There is no doubt that Our Lady taught Jacinta a great many things. Some of her prophecies, fulfilled exactly, cannot be explained otherwise than by divine intervention.

One day, Olímpia Marto, Jacinta's mother, had gone to visit her.

"Would you like it, Senhora Marto," the Mother Superior asked her, "if Florinda and Teresa [Jacinta's sisters] became nuns?"

"May the Lord not take them from me!" exclaimed the mother, who had a mistaken idea about the religious life and real love.

Jacinta had not heard anything of that conversation. Later, however, she said to the Mother Superior:

"Our Lady would like my sisters to be nuns, but

my mother doesn't want it. As a result, Our Lady will come soon and take them to heaven."

In fact, Florinda and Teresa died a few months afterwards.

On another occasion, she foretold the death of two doctors who had attended her very lovingly. Jacinta showed that she was very grateful to them. One day, one of them asked the little girl to recommend him to Our Lady.

"Yes," she said, nodding in assent. Then gazing at him, she added: "You will follow me soon."

To the other doctor, who asked her to pray for him and for his daughter, Jacinta promised and revealed the future to him too:

"You will follow me also, after your daughter. First she will die, then you."

There was a priest whom people considered zealous and pious. Jacinta said he was not living an exemplary life.

"How can that be?" people wondered, amazed at the statement.

"Soon they will all know for certain that it is true," she merely affirmed.

The facts, afterwards, proved her right.

Another time, she predicted to the Mother Superior that she would go to Fatima; she was very anxious to go but it was not possible just then.

"You will go to Fatima and to Madrid, but only after my death."

In fact, this prophecy was fulfilled also, as well as many others, which prove that Jacinta spoke through supernatural inspiration.

Last days

Meanwhile, she was taken to the Hospital D. Estefania to have an operation. She knew, and said, that she was going to die because Our Lady had told her the day and the time, but the doctor insisted she have the operation, and she submitted.

On 2 February 1920, after going to Confession and receiving Holy Communion, she went to the Tabernacle of the chapel to say goodbye to her 'Hidden Jesus', then left for the hospital accompanied by her good 'godmother'.

How different the surroundings were! Jacinta could say she was really alone if she had not had the company of two or three good people and her godmother.

On 10 February the painful operation took place. How many acts of renewed offering!

Jacinta was extremely weak and could not have an anaesthetic. Hence, she was aware of everything and suffered dreadfully; two of her ribs had to be removed from her left side, leaving a wound the size of a hand.

Who gave the little martyr the strength not to complain, even during such painful treatment? Such strength that she even smiled? It was Our Lady, whom she called on, full of confidence, and to whom she renewed her offering of every sacrifice.

"Patience," she said to herself when her suffering was at its most intense, "we all have to suffer in order to go to heaven."

And, later:

"Now I don't complain any more. Our Lady

appeared to me again, saying that she would come for me soon, and she took away all my pain."

Her bright face lit up with such a glowing expression that it seemed to reflect heaven itself.

The hours passed by. Jacinta knew when her time would come, since it had been revealed to her, and she awaited it eagerly.

In the company of the Angels

On the afternoon of Friday 20 February, the little girl said she was feeling very ill. She went to Confession for the last time, with angelic devotion. She asked for Holy Viaticum but it was deferred to the following day because her state did not seem to be as serious as she herself thought. A last precious sacrifice for her generous heart which was longing for Jesus in the Eucharist. Very soon, she would be in the eternal Communion of heaven!

For the last time she heard the clock striking: ten-thirty.

Darkness all around, the cold of winter… Strength was ebbing from the little body which was about to disintegrate. Jacinta's heartbeats became slower, ready to stop for ever.

At her bedside, there was just one nurse. Her mother, Lúcia, and all her dear ones were missing. Had Our Lady not told her that she would die all alone? And had she not accepted this bitter sacrifice?

She was alone, completely alone. But there, in a heavenly light, visible only to her eyes, soon to open to heavenly visions, Our Lady came and with love:

*cut off by the stem
this 'Portuguese Flower'
and took it to heaven ...*

Jacinta was just ten years old.

Clothed in her white First Communion dress, with a blue ribbon around her waist, she seemed to be showing the whole world the sublime ideal, which she had so heroically lived.

Prayer ... Love ... Sacrifice!

What would Jacinta do now?

Her soul infinitely whiter than her First Communion dress, Jacinta, a living flower, took, with Our Lady, the luminous road to heaven.

What was she going to do up there?

She told us herself, a few days before her death.

"I am going to love Our Lord and Our Lady very much," she told Lúcia; "to beg graces for you, for sinners, for the Holy Father, for my parents, for my brothers and sisters, and for everyone who asked my prayers."

One example is enough to give us some idea of the efficacy of her prayers.

An aunt of Lúcia's had a son who caused her great anxiety because of the way that he behaved. He had left home and nobody knew where he had gone.

The poor mother (who lived in Fatima) ran to

Lúcia's house in Aljustrel to ask for prayers. Not finding Lúcia, she recommended herself to Jacinta, who promised to pray.

Some days afterwards, the young man, pursued by the prayers of this innocent child, returned home, repentant and reformed. In Aljustrel, he spoke of his adventure:

"Having spent all the money I had stolen, I wandered for some time from one place to another, until (I don't remember exactly how it happened) I was jailed in Torres Novas. Soon afterwards, I managed to escape one night, and ran away through hills and valleys unknown to me. Thinking I was lost and afraid of being arrested again, I turned to God as my last hope. I knelt down and prayed. After a few minutes, Jacinta appeared to me, she took me by the hand and brought me to the main road, signing to me to keep going in that direction. When morning came, I recognised the place I was in, and, very relieved, I returned home."

But was it true that Jacinta had been with him that night?

The little seer said she didn't know those hills and woods but she affirmed that she had prayed and begged Our Lord to grant this request, through Our Lady's intercession.

Jacinta obtained her requests, because she knew how to give.

When someone learns how to carry out the Divine will, they gain power over the Heart of God himself, because the Lord cannot say "No" to those who answer "Yes" to him. He has, moreover, a weakness for those who, when they pray, do not go to him directly but – like Jacinta – make their requests through the hands of Mary. That is what the dear little shepherdess teaches us. Jacinta, who is in heaven in order to ask for graces and who, up there, awaits one more of those dear to her: her own Lúcia.

* * *

His Holiness John Paul II beatified Jacinta Marto and Francisco Marto on 13 May 2000 when he solemnly pronounced these words of beatification:

Gathered here at the expressed wish of our Brother Serafim, the Bishop of Leiria-Fatima, and many of our Brothers in the episcopate, and of all the faithful in Christ, and having heard of the findings of the Congregation for the Causes of Saints, with our apostolic Authority we agree that, from this day on, the Venerable Servants of God, Francisco Marto and Jacinta Marto, may be called Blessed and may have their feast celebrated each year, locally according to the norms of the privilege, on 20 February.

In the name of the Father and of the Son and of the Holy Spirit.